OXFORDSHIRE COUNTRY WALKS

4
UPPER THAMES
AND VALE

MARY WEBB   ALAN SPICER
ALLISTER SMITH

ILLUSTRATED BY LOUISE SPICER

OXFORDSHIRE BOOKS

First published in 1994 by Oxfordshire Books
Copyright © 1994 Oxfordshire County Council

British Library Cataloguing in Publication Data

Oxfordshire County Council
Oxfordshire Country Walks. – Vol. 4: Upper Thames and Vale
I. Title

ISBN 0-7509-0576-X

Library of Congress Cataloging in Publication Data applied for

Produced for
OXFORDSHIRE BOOKS
Official Publisher to Oxfordshire County Council
by
Alan Sutton Publishing Ltd
Phoenix Mill · Far Thrupp
Stroud · Gloucestershire

Cover photograph: River Thames near Rushey Lock (Alan Spicer)

Typeset in 10/12 Times.
Typesetting and origination by
Alan Sutton Publishing Limited
Printed in Great Britain by
Ebenezer Baylis & Son Limited
The Trinity Press, Worcester, and London

Contents

Preface

This series of circular walks explores part of the Vale of the White Horse, an area bordered by the Thames to the north and the Berkshire Downs to the south, between Lechlade to the west and Buckland to the east. Some of the walks include sections of the new Thames Path which follows the river to London.

The length of the walks varies from 3–9 miles (5–15 km) and short cuts are included where possible. Most of the walks are on level ground but in wet weather the terrain can be muddy. The time taken to follow the routes will depend on the individual, but the walks are designed to be taken at a leisurely pace to allow plenty of time to read the descriptions and look at the landscape and wildlife. Ordnance survey maps (1:25000) will add to the interest of the routes and grid reference numbers head each section of the descriptions.

The guide has been produced with the aim of showing how much of our history, both man-made and natural, is present in the landscape. You will find features such as the famous prehistoric White Horse, Iron Age camps, Saxon villages, remnants of medieval agriculture, enclosure landscapes and modern land use changes. The introduction gives a brief background to the history of the landscape and the wildlife of the area.

We hope you will enjoy discovering your landscape as much as we enjoyed producing this book.

Introduction

The region covered in these walks from the Thames to the Berkshire Downs has always been a rich agricultural area. However, at the time of writing, agricultural changes are in progress which may influence the appearance of the landscape, so making some of our comments inappropriate. The reduction in cereal production and the introduction on a large scale of 'set-aside' land will alter the appearance of the countryside and in turn affect the wildlife present. These changes are a timely reminder that landscape is not static and is constantly being altered by a variety of natural and human influences. Some of these have left their mark and can still be seen today.

GEOLOGY

The underlying geology of the area is quite varied and this variety has influenced the pattern of human use.

Various types of sediment were laid down millions of years ago when conditions were very different to the present time. For many millions of years this part of Europe was covered with seas. Earth movements altered the water depth which varied between oxygen-poor deep water to warm shallow seas, thus controlling the type of deposit which formed. Later, tilting and uplift caused by collision of continental plates formed the Berkshire Downs and also exposed other strata to erosion; consequently different rock types are now exposed at the surface as reflected in the diverse soil types present.

During the Upper Jurassic period (190–136 million years ago) at a time when the water was relatively deep, Oxford Clay was deposited, in some places up to 400 feet (100 m) in depth. This stratum is the oldest exposed in the region and occurs on the flatter land towards the River Thames. Slightly later, although still in the Jurassic Period, a patch of coral reefs formed when the seas were shallower, the remains of which make up the Corallian ridge on which Faringdon, Pusey and Buckland are situated. The sea levels then changed again, becoming deeper and the fine grained sediments deposited then are known as Kimmeridge Clay. Shellingford and Stanford-in-the-Vale are situated on this strata. The soils formed from Oxford and Kimmeridge Clays are sticky and heavy and would probably have been too weighty for early light ploughs to cultivate.

Just south of Faringdon lies a small outcrop of Lower Greensand which was laid down in a warm shallow sea during the early part of the Cretaceous period (136–64 million years ago). Contrary to its name it is not green; but the alternative name in this particular place of the 'Faringdon Sponge Gravel' is more descriptive as it contains abundant marine fossils, especially sponges. This gravel is quarried in the Faringdon district. The level land beneath the escarpment of the Berkshire Downs is formed from Gault Clay, deposited later in the Cretaceous period. This is found around Uffington and Woolstone where the soil is a characteristic grey colour. Although clay, the Gault is not so heavy as the Kimmeridge and Oxford clays. The Berkshire Downs themselves are of chalk, the most important deposit of the Cretaceous period and which gives this era its name, from 'creta', the Greek word for chalk.

Chalk is made up of the calcium carbonate skeletons of microscopic marine algae and is a porous and permeable rock which can hold much water. The water trickles through the numerous cracks and fissures in the rock until it reaches the impermeable layer of

Gault Clay beneath where it emerges in springs and streams at the foot of the escarpment. This line is called the springline and is marked by a string of villages which grew up there taking advantage of a steady water supply. Although much of the land would appear to be clay, in many places this is overlain by sands and gravels resulting from thousands of years of erosion by rain, wind and ice. These gravel terraces formed along the river valley and were often used for temporary settlements by prehistoric man. The most recent deposit in this region is the alluvium which lies along the riverbank. This layer results from flooding of the river which leaves silt, so producing a fine dark soil.

LANDSCAPE AND CHANGE

Early History

Prehistoric settlers tended to follow water courses, and evidence of this is shown by archaeological finds which are most numerous close to the River Thames and the River Ock. Later, Iron Age people have left a visible mark in the number of earthworks and forts on the hill tops (Walks 2, 5). Visible from many places along these walks the famous White Horse at Uffington is thought to date from the Iron Age, although experts are now investigating the possibility that it may be Saxon in origin. Romans again utilized land which was well watered, and several farms or villas were situated along the springline at the foot of the Downs at Fawler and Woolstone (Walk 6) and on the Corallian ridge with its lighter soil (Walk 3).

The Middle Ages

As the population slowly increased so more land was utilized, often in quite inhospitable places. Much of the Vale was very wet in the past and place names ending in 'ey' – an island as in Pusey – or 'ford' – as at Shellingford and Stanford – indicate this.

In the broad landscape of the Vale a system of

agriculture developed which was based on large open fields farmed in common by the village. Any marginal marshy or very poor land was commonland or 'waste' used for rough grazing and for gathering firewood. Land beside a water course was likely to be pasture or meadow for haymaking.

The arable land was divided into furlongs, further subdivided into strips, within two or three large fields. The strips, which were held by villagers, tenants of the lord of the manor, were scattered throughout the fields, so that everyone had a share of good or poor land. The same crops were grown on all the strips in a field, the crops rotating so that one year in two or three, one field would lie fallow and unsown to rest the land. The land was ploughed by teams of oxen in such a way that in time ridges and furrows developed. The crops were sown on the ridges and the furrows helped drainage, especially important where the land was wet. A strip would have been composed of several ridges. In the thirteenth century marginal land was cultivated as the population expanded, thus steep land on the escarpment of the Downs was ploughed into lynchets or terraces, remains of which can still be seen (Walk 6). However, this agricultural expansion was brought to a sudden end with a large drop in population caused by the Black Death in the fourteenth century, leaving this land uncultivated as pasture, so preserving the shape of the lynchets. Around this time there was an agricultural trend away from arable farming to sheep rearing for wool, which also resulted in ridge-and-furrow being preserved as the land was put down to grass (Walks 2, 5, 6).

Human habitation patterns have also changed over the centuries. Some settlements have become smaller like Inglesham and Woolstone (Walks 1, 6) while others have had a more drastic change in fortune. Baulking was important enough for a market to be held there in the thirteenth century but is now no more than a row of cottages (Walk 8). In all these places traces of the old settlement can be seen as bumps and hollows in the fields.

The Age of Improvement

The next major period of change came when landowners became interested in improving their yields and in trying new crops and methods. This spirit of change led to a movement towards enclosing the open fields, often without the consent of their tenants. During the eighteenth and ninteenth centuries all the open fields were enclosed and the new landscape laid out. Fields became smaller and more evenly shaped, edged with planted hawthorn or blackthorn hedges. Some hedges had existed earlier but these marked boundaries or perhaps the margins of the open fields or furlongs. The commonland was also brought into cultivation and now very little of this remains (Walks 4, 6). In some places the regular enclosure landscape is visible superimposed over the older ridge-and-furrow (Walks 2, 5). In other places the landowner altered the landscape for pleasure rather than profit. At Buckland Warren ornamental trees were planted over land which had previously been commonland (Walk 3), and at Buscot, Pusey and Buckland landscaped grounds were laid out over the old arable land (Walks 1, 7).

The Twentieth Century

In the twentieth century changes have occurred again. After the First World War the Forestry Commission was set up to promote self-sufficiency in timber. This led to plantations either adding to or replacing existing woodland (Walks 2, 5, 7). In the same way the Second World War led to a drive for self sufficiency in food. As machinery became larger, so hedges were removed to facilitate their use, and many of the enclosure hedges in this region have gone. Now, the process has gone full circle with land being set aside to reduce production of cereal, and hedges being replanted in some places.

AGRICULTURE AND CHANGE

A major landowner in the Vale of the White Horse was the Church. From the tenth century, Abingdon Abbey owned land further west around Uffington, Fawler, Pusey and Buckland for several centuries. Much of the land around Great Coxwell and other manors was owned in the thirteenth century by Beaulieu Abbey, a Cistercian monastery in Hampshire. These landowners were well organized and made the most of the rich agricultural land. By the time of the Domesday Book in 1086, the area was well known for its dairy produce, cheese being mentioned in several entries as a taxable item. This commodity was produced in large quantities until the twentieth century, with several thousand tons being transported to London annually. The typical regional cheese was similar to a single Gloucester but there were also local variations. A farm near Buscot produced a 'pineapple' cheese, so called because of the markings made by the mesh of the nets in which it dried. At Stanford-in-the-Vale the local cheese was shaped like a hare and flavoured with sage.

When transport became faster by railway, milk was the main produce, much going to the biscuit factory in Reading, as well as to London.

With the emphasis on livestock, it is not surprising that new breeds were developed in the area. In the nineteenth century around the Faringdon area, the Oxford Down sheep was developed from Southdown crossed with Cotswold and Hampshire Down. One of the most famous flocks belonged to Robert Hobbs of Kelmscott who also kept a pedigree herd of Shorthorn cattle.

Other agricultural innovations were developed in the region during the eighteenth and nineteenth centuries. Edward Loveden ran the model estate at Buscot (Walk 1) and developed a special plough to help drainage in the wet ground. He made use of the plentiful water supply by turning his meadows into water-meadows. Special water channels and drains were constructed which allowed the land to be covered with water in the winter, then drained in early spring. This process kept the soil warm and encouraged the new spring grass to grow quickly, thus providing early feed for his cattle.

TRANSPORT AND CHANGE

The River Thames

Over the centuries the River Thames has been the focus of this region, being a major transport route for thousands of years. Early settlers must have used it to move into the area when the land was covered with forests and marshes.

Above Oxford, in its natural state, the river could be forded in places but weirs were constructed as early as Saxon times to back up the water to give enough power for water mills. The deeper water also increased the number of fish and eels, so giving rise to fisheries. Weirs also increased water depth where previously there had been shallows or rapids, so if carefully sited they could improve navigation along the river. Boats passed through a central removable section of the weir. The section would be taken out bit by bit and the boats would shoot down on the rush of water. Vessels going

River Thames below Buscot Lock

upstream would be hauled through the opening by horses or a winch. Tolls at weirs tended to be very high as often they were close to mills which needed the water for the mill wheel and the sluices were opened at the whim of the miller.

Modern 'pound' locks enable boats to move up and down the river while maintaining a sufficient level of water in all parts of the waterway. When the lock gates are opened only the water within the lock itself is lost rather than the flash of water which occurred in the old weir system. The first pound locks on the Thames were built in the seventeenth century. Along this stretch of the river they were not constructed until the late eighteenth century, after pressure from the owners of the Thames & Severn Canal.

Much goods traffic was carried by the river, although the size of the barges was dictated by the narrow arches of some of the bridges. Stone from quarries at Taynton seems to have been one of the major goods for transport throughout the history of river traffic, but grain, wool and cheese were also taken to London with an upstream trade in sea coal and luxury goods from the capital.

Canals

During the latter part of the eighteenth century a further expansion in the use of the Thames was brought about by the building of canals which linked the river network. The Thames & Severn Canal opened in 1789, linking these two rivers and allowing access to London for goods from South Wales and the West Midlands. It joined the Thames at Inglesham at the highest navigable point on the river which could be reached by 70-ton barges. Coal for local use was off-loaded at Lechlade, Buscot and Radcot but coal for Oxford came down the Oxford Canal. Grain and wool travelled west but much of the hoped-for trade did not appear. In 1810 the wider Kennet & Avon Canal opened and this drew much of the London–Bristol traffic. The route was shorter and had fewer locks, so making the journey far easier. The Thames & Severn Canal had always had problems with water leakage, as much of its route passed over porous Cotswold limestone, and this led to its decline. Some repairs were carried out at the end of the nineteenth century but the canal finally closed in 1927. The Wiltshire & Berkshire Canal opened in 1810, linking the Kennet & Avon Canal to the River Thames at Abingdon. This canal was never very profitable, although a wharf was built by Edward Loveden of Buscot for storing cheese prior to transport to London. The traffic on this canal was drastically affected by the opening of the Great Western Railway in 1840, and after many years of decline the owners finally closed the canal in 1910.

Today the traffic on the Thames is confined to pleasure craft, commercial activity having ceased after the Second World War.

Roads

Roads and paths evolved over the centuries following routes which were perhaps drier than the neighbouring land or which had a good view of the surrounding landscape to avoid ambush or attack. Although not covered by the walks in this book, one of the oldest routes in England runs along the top of the Downs. The Ridgeway dates back to prehistoric times, evolving as a route on the dry uplands along which stone for tools and, later, precious metals were carried. There is no record of a Roman road in this region but as there was Roman occupation then roads must have been present.

During the Middle Ages permanent stone bridges were built over the Thames in this region, earlier than downstream. The first reference to a stone bridge at Radcot dates from AD 958, although this would have been a simple one made of flat stone slabs laid on stone piers. This bridge provision reflects the busy trade in wool from the Cotswolds which was carried by pack-horse to the Channel ports for export to the Continent.

Big improvements were made to roads in the eighteenth century with the advent of the Turnpike Trusts. These were set up by private investors to improve the state of the roads and to make a profit from the tolls which they charged. Earlier the roads had been the responsibility of the parish and upkeep had been generally poor. The Lechlade-Swindon Trust not only improved the road surface but at Lechlade built a new road and bridge to ease traffic congestion at the old bridge. Gradually many roads were turnpiked and road transport improved.

Some routes were part of long cross-country networks. From the Middle Ages drove roads led from Wales to markets in London and the south-east. In this region such roads led through Lechlade and Faringdon to cross the Thames at Goring and go from there via High Wycombe to Barnet or to Kent via Reading. Another drove road led through Uffington following the line of the foot of the Downs escarpment.

Today, changes still occur with old routes being improved or new sections of road being constructed such as the relatively new Faringdon bypass.

Many of the paths which are used by walkers or riders today were more important in the past. The paths linked villages and churches and also led out of the villages to the open fields. Old maps, such as that made by John Rocque in 1761, show some present-day tracks or paths to be as important as roads, but changing needs and usage have reduced their status over the years. This is one reason why it is important to preserve the line of old paths, as they are direct links with past human use of the land.

NATURAL HISTORY

The countryside of this part of Oxfordshire is essentially agricultural and has been for many hundreds of years. However, although at first glance there seems to be little opportunity for wildlife, there are many places which provide a variety of habitats.

Heron

Rivers

The River Thames is a managed river. The channel is kept open for boats, locks and weirs maintain water level, and the erosion of banks is kept to a minimum. In contrast the River Ock and the various streams that run through the area are more natural, with only small-scale management to prevent silting. All these waterways contain running water which supports a wildlife community different to that found in still water such as ponds. Many plants and animals have adapted to cope with the speed of the flowing water. Others have evolved to live in conditions specific to their position, either on the riverbank or actually submerged in the water. Rivers and streams also act as wildlife corridors as it not easy to cultivate right up to the water's edge. These corridors can link one area of wildlife value with another, so allowing movement of species and colonization which would otherwise be difficult in an agricultural landscape.

Woodland

Due to its long history as an agricultural area, woodland is sparse in this region, with only two large woods to be seen on the walks. One of these woods at Buckland (Walks 3 and 7) was planted only about two hundred years ago, although the other, Coxwell Wood – now called Oak Wood – (Walk 2), is likely to be much older. There are many small patches however, some left as remnants of old woods or commonland, and others fairly recently planted such as at Pusey (Walk 7). Farmers are being encouraged to plant small patches of woodland on field corners to increase habitats for wildlife and to act as cover for game birds such as pheasant.

Woods provide a particular habitat for plants, animals and birds. Over time woods are fairly stable, allowing special plants which either colonize slowly or need undisturbed conditions to thrive. Bluebells fall into this latter category. They can grow well in the open but cannot tolerate disturbance so are usually found in woodland.

The planted evergreen conifers which grow in the

15

two large wooded areas tend to shade out most plants except at the woodland edge but can offer refuge and food to birds, especially in the winter. They are also a good habitat for fungi, several of which are closely associated with conifers.

Hedges

Many hedges in this region are only two hundred years old at the most, resulting from the enclosures of the eighteenth and nineteenth centuries. Although these 'new' hedges contain a limited number of shrub and tree species in comparison to older hedges, they are still valuable wildlife habitats. They provide food and shelter for birds, insects and small mammals, and, where the farmer leaves uncultivated verges, a site for flowering plants as well. They also act as corridors across agricultural land, allowing plants and animals to spread or colonize new land.

Fields

Most modern grassy fields have been improved by fertilizer and weed-killer applications, so drastically reducing their population of wild flowers. However,

Purple loosestrife

A vale cottage

Woodland toadstool

in some places in the area covered by these walks it is possible to see fields where some flowers still grow. Wide drainage ditches at the field edge also often provide a site for flowers. Increasingly land is being 'set aside' in a bid to reduce surplus grain production. These fields are left unsown and, as a result, wild plants start to colonize the land, the species partly depending on the existing seed-bank in the ground. Other species are those known as colonizers which spread from wind-blown seed and are the first to take over bare ground. The growth of such plants will encourage a whole variety of seed-eating birds which in recent decades have suffered a decline in numbers because of the decrease in suitable habitat and food supply.

══	Road
▬ ▬ ▬ ▬	Circular Walk
▬□▬□▬	Walk on road
───	Track
- - - -	Footpath
∿∿∿	Stream or River
⬭	Pond or lake
■	Building
▨	Residential
🌳	Deciduous trees
🌲	Conifers
⌐	Grassland
+	Church
PH	Public House
NT	National Trust
⊦⊦⊦⊦⊦	Railway line
Spr	Spring
FB	Footbridge
SC	Short cut
AR	Alternative route

Key to individual route maps

17

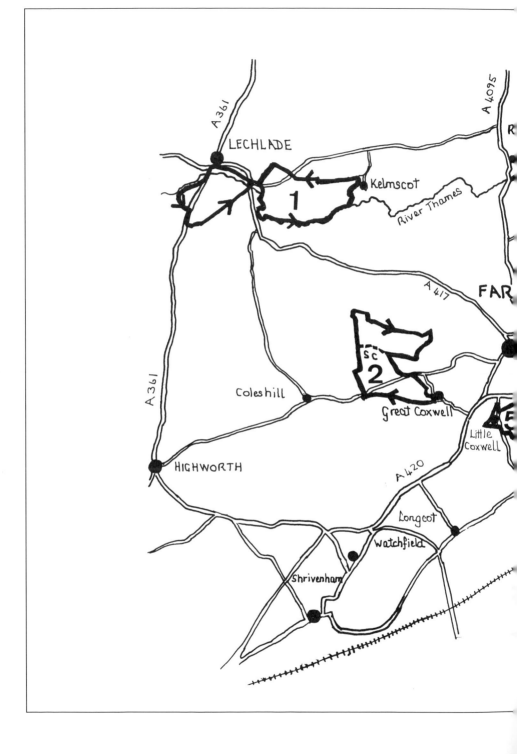

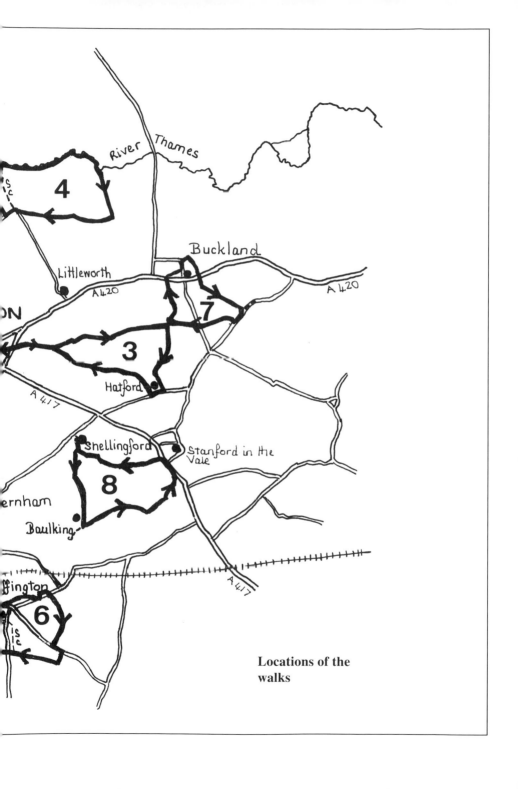

Locations of the walks

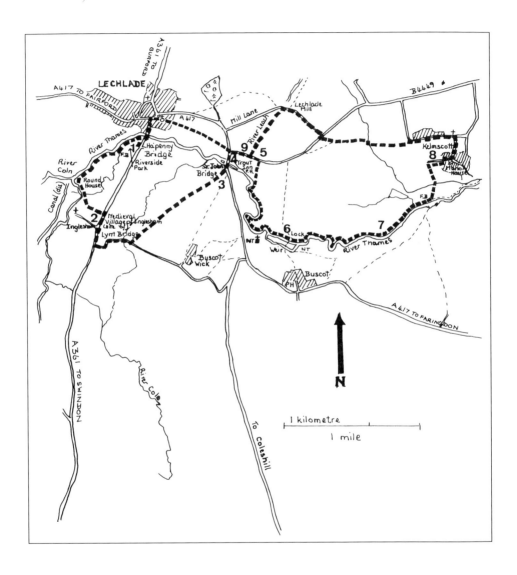

WALK 1

Lechlade

9 miles 15 km

Short cuts 3.5 miles 5 km and 5 miles 8 km

This route passes through three counties: Oxfordshire, Gloucestershire and Wiltshire. Much of it follows the riverbank but it also leads through the site of a deserted medieval settlement and Kelmscott, the home of William Morris.

The walk forms a figure of eight so can easily be split into two shorter walks. For a short walk start at Point 1 and follow the directions in the text. For a slightly longer alternative walk, turn to Point 4 to start and end there.

1   SU212993

Start from the large free car-park just out of Lechlade on the A361 Swindon road. Walk over the grass to the river and bridge, then turn left keeping the river on your right.

Notice how uniform this grass parking area is with very few flowering plants. The few dandelions and daisies have low-growing rosettes of leaves which avoid being cut. Grass grows from the base of the plant so when the long leaves are cut the plant is not damaged, hence its universal use for lawns. The bridge is called Ha'penny Bridge from the toll which had to be paid by pedestrians when it was first built around

Ha'penny Bridge, Lechlade

1792. The bridge and road were constructed to reduce the congestion in the town brought about by the extra traffic generated by the Thames & Severn Canal which joined the Thames close by. The arch was designed to allow river traffic easy passage, as the barges were towed by horses or men pulling ropes attached to masts at the front of the vessels.

Turn left and follow the riverbank for some distance.

On the river are mallard ducks which at some time have mated with white domestic birds. These ducks are accustomed to people and will swim towards you hoping for food. This is in marked contrast to the wild mallards further along the river which are very shy and avoid humans.

The path leads to a foot-bridge over a small stream which marks the boundary between Wiltshire and Gloucestershire. The channel is likely to be full of plants which like wet conditions; look out for iris, water forget-me-not, fool's watercress and great water dock. The riverbanks are very different as they are kept clear for boats and mooring stations.

Sandpiper

Continuing along the riverbank there are several small beaches, and you may be lucky enough to see a sandpiper, really a coastal bird which likes shallow water for feeding. You can identify it by its long legs, shrill call and its low flight. The fields are good feeding grounds for water fowl, especially in winter. Large flocks of Canada and greylag geese, and mute swans congregate here to graze on the grass.

Just past a wooden arched foot-bridge over the river you will see the Round House marking the entrance to the Thames & Severn Canal. This spot also marks the start of the navigable section of the River Thames for larger boats and the point where the River Coln joins the Thames. The canal opened in 1789, although the idea of linking the Thames with the Severn had been thought of during the early part of the eighteenth century. The barges carried industrial goods from the Midlands such as iron, copper, tin, bombshells and nails, while traffic from London brought groceries, foreign timber and other merchandise. Coal from the Staffordshire mines was one of the most important cargoes but the opening of the Grand Union Canal in

23

The Round House, Inglesham

1800 gave a more direct link with the Midlands, so reducing the importance of the Thames & Severn Canal. The final blow for this canal came with the opening of the Great Western Railway in 1841 between London and Bristol. This provided quicker and cheaper transport, and over the next decades the canal gradually fell into disrepair, finally closing in 1927.

The Round House was one of several along the canal used by lock-keepers and watchmen. Note the weeping willow in the garden. This tree belongs to the same family as the willows lining the riverbank here. These so-called crack willows have been pollarded, i.e. their crowns have been removed to prevent the large heavy branches from falling and splitting the trunk which would then decay. New growth results from pollarding, so in the past this was done on a regular basis both to preserve the tree and to produce usable poles.

Follow the path along the river until you reach a

small metal bridge over a ditch. Cross this and, bearing left away from the river, continue through the field making for a stile in the hedge ahead. The bumps in this field are all that remains of a medieval village called Inglesham. The unspoiled eleventh-century church still stands. William Morris helped with its repair in 1888 and so prevented any large-scale alterations.

2 SU208984

Cross over the stile onto the main road and turn right. Take the first turn on the left signposted to Buscot. Walk with care for about 440 yards (400 m) as the traffic is fast.

Once in the lane you will notice the rich variety of shrub species in the left-hand hedge which indicates its age; this hedge was shown on a map of Berkshire made in 1761. It contains spindle, hawthorn, crab-apple, field maple, blackthorn, willow and elder. A little further on look at the plants growing on the stone wall near the farm. Stonecrop has thick fleshy leaves to store water, an essential feature on a wall where the soil is almost non-existent and conditions can be very dry.

The lane crosses Lynt Bridge over a branch of the River Cole. Pause here to look at the plants growing close to the water, some of which have been used by man for centuries. Comfrey grows here; its flowers may be purple, pink or white and are much loved by bumble-bees. This plant is well known in herbal medicine and is recommended for blood and heart disorders and many other ailments. Nettles can be used as a vegetable when young; the plant also contains fibres which can be used to produce thread. Willows have also proved useful to man; the active ingredient in aspirin was first extracted from them.

Just past a bend in the road, go through a small metal gate on the left and take the byway which crosses a field in line with the telegraph poles. Follow the track for one mile (1.5 km). This follows the route of the old Swindon road which, before the construction of Ha'penny Bridge, used the only bridge out of

Lechlade, St John's Bridge, which you will cross soon. This old road fell into disuse when the turnpike was opened in 1793 which followed the route of the present busy main road seen earlier.

As you walk through the agricultural fields notice the lack of variety in the flowers among the crops compared to the verges along the edges. Modern chemicals can eliminate 'weeds' which in the past competed with the crops, often reducing yields drastically. Cereal fields are another type of grassland; others seen already along this walk were the mown recreation ground and the lush growth in the pasture or silage fields. These cereals are grown for their seeds, the grain. These have been selected by plant breeders to be large and to remain in the seed-head when ripe, unlike wild grasses which shed the ripe seeds very readily.

Elder bushes in the hedgerows have healthy growths of lichen on the branches and trunk. Look for three forms: orange leaf-like growth (foliose), grey cement-like (crustose), and the branched fruticose form so-called because it produces red reproductive structures on the tips of its branches. Lichens are an intimate mix of fungus and algae which help each other to feed and survive. They are generally very sensitive to pollution so disappear quickly in polluted places; some types are now used as indicators of environmental quality.

To the left in the distance is a fine view of Lechlade church with its prominent spire, while the woodland on the hilltop to the right is in Buscot Park, now owned by the National Trust.

Further along this section the track leads along the right-hand edge of a double hedge, very clear remnants of the old road. Between the hedges the ground is obviously quite damp. In May there are clumps of bright yellow marsh marigolds here, the largest flower of the buttercup family, hence its other name of kingcups. A third name is May blobs which describes both the flowering time and the shape of the large unopened buds. Look out for the rabbit warren, conspicuous with the short grazed vegetation and bare scratched earth with few tall plants.

Marsh marigold

3 SU222989

Go through a gate and cross the field to a stile and foot-bridge over a ditch. At the road turn left to St John's Bridge.

There are some interesting plants in the ditch. Look for two members of the cow-parsley or umbellifer family. Wild angelica, a close relative of the culinary angelica, has smooth, purple stems while the very poisonous hemlock has purple blotched stems. The leaves of hemlock are more finely divided than those of angelica and this is also a distinguishing feature. It would be wise not to touch either though, just in case!

Another plant which is especially noticeable in spring, with small white flowers and bright green leaves, is hedge mustard. The leaves smell strongly of cabbage if crushed and in fact this plant belongs to the cabbage family. Orange-tip butterflies lay their bright orange eggs close to the flowers. The caterpillars feed on the long seed pods and are well camouflaged as they are a similar long, thin shape. They only eat the leaves when there is no alternative available.

There has been a bridge here for many centuries. The last wooden one was washed away in 1203 and within a few years was replaced by a stone bridge and causeway, King John contributing 50 marks towards its cost. Almshouses for the men working on the bridge were provided by Isabella de Ferrers who owned the manor of Lechlade. In time these became the Priory of St John the Baptist, so giving the bridge its name. The priory was responsible for the upkeep of the bridge with its total of twenty-six arches, but local and national turmoil over the following centuries left the bridge in a bad state of repair. During the sixteenth century the remains of the abandoned priory were used to repair the bridge but later that century the bridge was reported again to be in poor state. In 1646 a Civil War skirmish took place close to the bridge and the dead were buried on the old Berkshire side of the river (the south bank). When the Thames & Severn Canal was being planned it was decided to alter St John's Bridge to allow for the larger boats and loads expected. A

St John's Lock

new straight channel was made on the south of the bridge, crossed by a new single-span bridge linked to the old bridge by a causeway. By the middle of the nineteenth century the old bridge was beyond further repair and a new one was finished in 1886.

For a closer look at the lock and bridge, go through a wooden gate on the left and down a flight of steps. By the lock-keeper's house is a statue of old Father Thames, transferred from the source of the river at Thameshead. The lock is the furthest upstream on the Thames.

4 SU223991

Over the bridge, cross the road and take the turning to the right, alongside the Trout Inn, signposted to Kelmscott.

For a shorter walk returning directly to Lechlade take the tarmac path on the left opposite the road to Kelmscott. Turn to Point 9.

For a longer alternative route, start and end here at the Trout Inn, following Points 4 to 8.

Father Thames

Guelder rose lines the banks of the small stream on the right-hand side of the road. Its creamy-white flowers form flat clusters, the outer flowers having much larger petals than the others. In autumn rich red berries are produced which are poisonous. This shrub is related to the familiar garden snowball tree but the garden variety is sterile. The vegetation along the stream is quite sparse because of the heavy shading from the trees, although in early spring before the leaves are out there is a thick carpet of bright yellow lesser celandine. The shiny leaves die back quickly after flowering. In wetter places look out for water mint and the blue-flowered brooklime together with yellow marsh marigold.

5 SU226991

Cross the bridge spanning the River Leach which gives Lechlade its name. Look over the left-hand

29

parapet of the bridge to see three kinds of fern – maidenhair, common polypody and hart's tongue – growing on the garden walls. They are all native to Britain but rare in this part of the Thames valley.

After about a quarter of a mile (0.5 km) you will reach a track on the right just before a house called Waterways. Go through the small gate and follow the track through a second gate.

The trees lining the track are poplars, often planted as a windbreak. Some of the leaves may have large bumps on their stalks caused by an aphid, which produces a cancerous growth making the stalk twist and swell to form a cavity where the aphid reproduces.

Climb over a stile, then turn left along the riverbank. Follow the riverside path to Buscot Lock.

Although the fields bordering the river are used for agriculture and the river in many places has been dredged, there is still plenty to see along the banks. The vegetation close to the water's edge favours a wet habitat. Alder trees grow here, their roots helping to hold the bank together. The wood is resistant to rotting and in the past was used for making clogs and broomheads, and other items which regularly get wet. Two members of the cabbage family can also be seen along the bank. Mauve lady's smock and yellow cress both have four petals arranged in a cross shape, hence the scientific name of crucifers for this group. All this family are non-poisonous and many are used as vegetables, e.g. cabbage, watercress and mustard. You may also find the large pink flowers of Himalayan balsam which has spread along the banks of many waterways since its introduction to this country during the last century. The large seed-pods have tensioned edges and explode, throwing out their seeds, if you touch or pinch them, hence another name for the plant is touch-me-not.

Animals are also present along the riverbank. Holes near water level are likely to be the homes of water-voles, commonly called water-rats – the Ratty of *Wind in the Willows*. These inoffensive rodents live on succulent stems of bankside plants, and worms and

Himalayan balsam

snails from the riverbed. Insects to look out for are
dark brown stone flies which perch on the vegetation
in early May, followed later in the summer by
brilliantly coloured damselflies and dragon-flies. All
these insects have a dense network of veins in their
wings; this is regarded as a primitive feature compared
to the few parallel veins of butterflies and bees.

Human influences can also be seen along the river.
The large concrete structures are pillboxes built early
in the Second World War in case of a river invasion.
Across the river is a grassy area owned by the National
Trust where a busy wharf and warehouses once stood;
corn and cheese was brought from upstream and the
surrounding area for shipment on larger barges to
London. Up to the end of the nineteenth century the
Vale of the White Horse was famous for its cheeses
which were similar to single Gloucester but with many
local variations.

6   SU230981

Soon the path reaches Buscot Lock and weir. Continue
along the riverbank.

Water is taken from the river here and, after
filtration and treatment, is suitable for drinking. In
modern times the demand for water from the river for
agricultural, domestic and industrial use, often in
places far from the river, has resulted in drastic falls in
water levels, and dried-up tributaries.

The weir is likely to have been in existence for far
longer than the lock; weirs were constructed as early
as Saxon times to back up the water to give enough
power for water-mills. This pound lock was built as
part of the improvements to the river carried out in
preparation for the opening of the Thames & Severn
Canal at the end of the eighteenth century (see
Introduction).

Continue past a bridge, following the river
downstream.

Mute swans may nest here, the nest being a mound
up to 6½ feet (2 m) in diameter made of reeds and

Mute swan on nest

other vegetation. Further downstream beyond Henley, the swans are either owned by the Crown, the Vintners Company or the Dyers Company, but here these rules do not apply. Black-headed gulls are often to be seen in the Thames valley in winter, especially when the fields are ploughed as they feed on insects. However, at this time of the year they are often unrecognized as their chocolate-brown heads turn white.

As you walk, notice the soil in the field close to the river. It is fine alluvial soil mixed with gravel left behind by the river over centuries of flooding. On a larger scale the river has formed wide terraces. During cold periods as the Ice Age gradually ended, the river carried large amounts of debris, resulting from the weathering and freezing of rocks, which was deposited in the river valley. During warmer periods when there was very little deposit the river tended to cut a channel through the previous deposits, so leaving a terrace. Four such terraces have been identified in the Upper Thames valley.

As you walk along the river you will have noticed how it follows a winding course. These curves are called meanders and are formed as the river erodes material on the outside of a bend where the current is fastest and deposits material on the inside curve so gradually resulting in the riverbed moving sideways in larger and larger bends.

7 SU240982

Continue alongside the river for a mile (1.5 km). As you draw level with a small patch of woodland on the right of the river, notice the hedge line curving away from the river. This line of willows follows a stream which marks the parish boundary between Eaton Hastings and Buscot. Its sinuous line contrasts with the regular shape of nearby fields. Most parish boundaries date from antiquity and often follow water courses and other natural features. A group of magnificent pollarded poplars can be seen each side of a large foot-bridge across the river; they mark the site of Hart's weir which used to have the greatest fall of water on the upper river, over 4 feet (1.3 m) in periods of low water.

When you reach the foot-bridge, look out for a path on the left leading away from the river. Follow this path keeping the fence on your left. At the end of the field, climb the stile and cross the foot-bridge. Follow the path ahead up the next field. At the top of the field, turn right along a path between two hedges and continue to the road.

This village is Kelmscott, famous as the home of William Morris who rented a house here from 1871. William Morris was a designer of tapestries, wallpaper, furniture and books, a poet and writer, and an early socialist. He lived here with his wife Jane and other members of the Pre-Raphaelite Arts and Crafts Movement, particularly Dante Gabriel Rossetti. Morris died in 1896 and is buried in the churchyard here. The house contains many relics of the movement and is open to visitors on the first Wednesday of the month.

8 SU249991

Turn left along the road (right to see Kelmscott
Manor), then left at the road junction. The church on
the right along this road is worth a visit. A little further
along the road the stone wall supports a fine collection
of ferns and flowering plants adapted to its harsh
environment. Look for wall pennywort, whose Latin
name *Umbilicus* refers to the alternative name of
navelwort, all three descriptive of the leaf shape. At a
right-hand bend in the road past the end of the village,
take the track which continues straight on through a
wide expanse of fields. When a stream is reached turn
right and follow it to a foot-bridge on the left which
the path crosses.

This stream is another example of a boundary, this
time not only a parish boundary between Lechlade and
Kelmscott but also the county boundary between
Gloucestershire and Oxfordshire. The deep channel is
several feet below the level of the surrounding land
and the banks provide a habitat for several water-
loving plants. Meadowsweet has creamy fragrant
flowers in summer; the leaves were used as floor
covering in the past, giving a pleasant aroma when
trodden on. Fluffy pink heads of hemp agrimony can
also be seen here, so named because of its resemblance
to hemp or cannabis.

In the next field go straight on to meet the edge of a
hedge and continue in the same direction to the field
corner. Climb the stile and keep going with the hedge
on your right. Through the next gate, cross the field to
a gate on the right of the Dutch barn and go through
onto the road. Here turn right, then left down a narrow
lane marked 'weak bridge' which leads to Lechlade
Mill. Go past Mill Cottage then turn left along the
edge of the River Leach, walking past industrial units
over a concrete yard to a stile in the far corner.

Notice the clumps of moss growing at the river's
edge. These primitive plants are dependent on water to
keep them healthy for photosynthesis and reproduction
and, for these reasons, are often found in cool damp
places. You may also see trout in the clear water; they

Meadowsweet

need cool flowing water containing plenty of oxygen so will not be seen in polluted or still water.

Follow the river, keeping it on your left, and climb three more stiles until you reach the road.

Notice the closely grazed fields. The only large plants which survive are those with defences such as prickles (thistles), stinging hairs (nettles) or a bitter taste (docks). These defences, however, don't protect against small insects which are not bothered by them.

9 SU225992

Turn right and walk back along the road towards the Trout Inn.

This is the end of the longer alternative route.

The short route continues from this point.

Cross the main road with care and take the tarmac path opposite, known as Shelley's Walk, after the poet who spent some time at Lechlade in the early nineteenth century.

The shrubs here produce autumn berries for birds and small mammals. The wild privet produces clusters of strong-smelling white flowers, followed in the autumn by small black berries which are eaten by starlings. The riverside fields are good locations for flocks of geese which are easily observed through gaps in the hedges.

The path leads back to Lechlade across fields and through the churchyard. Take the road ahead through the town, turning left at the traffic lights. Continue to Ha'penny Bridge, then turn right down steps into the grassy Riverside Park and return to the car-park.

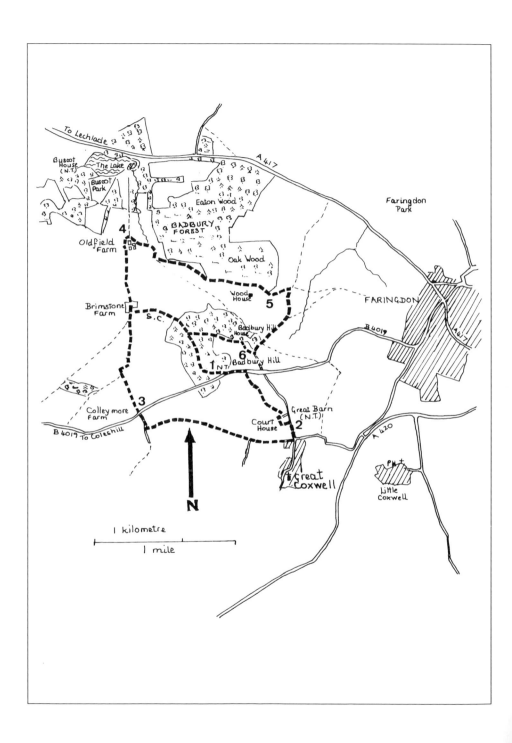

Great Coxwell

6.5 miles   10.5 km

Short cut 4 miles 6.5 km

This walk passes through countryside which still bears the marks of past generations, ranging from Iron Age earthworks, medieval agriculture, and more recent enclosure and forestry. Parts of the route can be muddy. A short cut may be taken (see Point 3).

1   SU262946

Start at the National Trust car-park at Badbury Hill. Walk out of the car-park to the road and turn left for a short distance. Be careful of fast-moving traffic. After about 220 yards (200 m), take the footpath which leads off to the right and follow this downhill.

In the car-park area you may see chaffinches which fly down for titbits from visitors; the males are quite pink, much brighter than the females, though both have a small crest on their heads. Other birds are likely to be heard if not seen in this area. Skylarks nest on the ground in the surrounding fields and sing as they soar high into the sky, becoming silent as they come down to the ground again. Yellowhammers live in the hedgerows. The male sings from hedge-tops or telegraph wires, the song commonly described as saying 'A little bit of bread and no cheese'.

When you are safely off the road, pause and look at

the view. Ahead in the far distance are the Berkshire Downs, and you should be able to see the White Horse on the hillside above Uffington. This is thought to date from the Iron Age over 2,000 years ago and could have been a tribal symbol as there are the remnants of a large settlement on the hilltop. Badbury Hill, on which you are standing, was the site of an Iron Age fort with circular banks and ditches much levelled in the nineteenth century. Finds of pottery and worked flints from the Mesolithic and Neolithic periods (6,000 and 4,000 years ago) show that the area was inhabited even earlier than this. The hill provides a good vantage point with views to the north over a large expanse of the upper Thames valley. In autumn and winter the cold air sinks to the valley bottom. Low-lying mists contrast with sunlit hilltops and produce very photogenic landscapes.

Continue along the path, turning left over a stile into a small plantation.

Poplars have been planted in this moist hollow, fast-growing trees which favour damp conditions. Other plants which also like the cool shade can be seen. Large-leaved burdock produces seeds with stiff bristly hooks which easily stick to clothes or animal fur, so ensuring widespread dispersal. A large patch of rosebay willow-herb grows here. The tall spikes of pink flowers produce blue pollen which is much liked by bees and can be seen as large pollen balls attached to their hind legs when they have been visiting the flowers. The old elderberry bushes beneath the trees will have been brought here as seeds deposited in bird droppings. A wetter patch as you leave the plantation encourages great willow-herb which often grows in wet ditches. The spiky leafless stems of *Juncus* rush grow here too. Although it might be thought that these spikes are the leaves of the plant, flowers are produced on them, showing that in fact they are stems.

Follow the path over a foot-bridge and a stile, then turn left along the field edge.

Ahead is Great Coxwell Barn but before reaching it look at the plants growing on the edge of the cereal

The Great Barn, Great Coxwell

field. (The crop may vary from year to year but you will be sure to see cereals somewhere along this route.) These so-called 'weeds of cultivation' grow on regularly disturbed soils such as fields or gardens. They cannot survive where the vegetation is thick as in hedgerows or grasslands. Field pansy, field speedwell, mayweed and shepherd's purse all grow quickly in the spring, flowering and developing seed when still quite small. The seeds can remain dormant for many years if covered by ploughing but when brought to the surface again soon germinate and start a new cycle. Poppies are another such plant; the red verges along new road developments show the presence of the seed-bank lying dormant until the right conditions occur.

Take the stile left towards the barn.

The Great Barn dates from the latter half of the thirteenth century and was built as part of a Cistercian monastic grange for the then Berkshire estates of the Abbey of Beaulieu. A grange was the administrative centre of an estate and contained many buildings to house the people to run it and to store the produce and equipment. The monks owned property in the Faringdon area and it is thought that the barn may have been built to house the tithes of the churches of Inglesham (see Walk 1) and Shilton which the abbey took over in 1243. Originally the farms were worked by lay brothers of the Cistercian order but gradually local people were employed. By the fourteenth century there was a large workforce including ploughmen, carters, a hayward, a forester, a baker and cheesemaker and a swineherd. The large doors in the end walls of the Great Barn were made in the eighteenth century; originally they opened on the east and west sides. The produce was brought in through these doors and stacked at each end of the barn, leaving the centre area free as workspace. During the winter the harvest was threshed by hand so that grain was removed from oats, barley and wheat, or pulses from peas and beans. The grain would then be taken for milling or to market and the straw used for bedding.

At the dissolution of the monasteries in 1538 the grange including the barn came into the possession of the Mores family. The present-day Court House is likely to be the site of the grange but the Great Barn is all that is left of this once busy centre. The barn is a Grade I listed building and ancient monument owned by the National Trust. Its unique historical and architectural importance was recognized a century ago by William Morris who lived nearby and often took visitors to see it (see Walk 1).

Outside the barn there is also plenty of interest. Look up to see the dovecot over the east door. Domesticated doves were used for food in the past but now the barn provides nesting sites for jackdaws and pigeons as well. The pond is bordered by willows which are pollarded every so often. The tops of the trees are cut off and from the stumps new branches grow, so regenerating the trees. This is the traditional method of managing willows which otherwise would get top heavy, split open and rot. The pond is also home to water-snails which live on the weed and to the larvae of dragon-flies and damselflies. The adults can be seen flying in the vicinity during the summer. The damselflies are blue and black, and their wings close over their backs when at rest. Dragon-flies hold their wings horizontally and tend to be larger in size.

2 SU269940

Leaving the barn turn right along the road and walk through the village until you reach Puddleduck Lane on the right.

Notice the plants growing on the drystone walls. They are all adapted to withstand the harsh dry conditions. Mosses grow slowly, and in hot dry conditions can cut down their chemical activity so that they are not harmed. Two ferns to look out for are wall rue and rusty-back fern; both are evergreens and have tough leaves to withstand desiccation. Stonecrop and wall-flowers can also be seen, probably garden escapees which have found a habitat similar to their natural environment. Ivy also covers many of the walls, and in autumn the greenish flowers attract many bees, wasps and flies.

Turn right down Puddleduck Lane and continue past the houses and through the fields along a track.

The hedgerow on the right is rich in both shrubs and flowering species. The hedge contains crab-apple, field maple, hawthorn, blackthorn, hazel, elder, dogwood and dogrose. This large number of species probably indicates a very old hedge, and certainly this track is shown on a map of Berkshire made in 1761. Further along look out for the gnarled remains of old ash and field maples which were 'laid' many years ago to thicken the hedge.

Many flowers can be seen all through the spring and summer. Bluebells and cowslips in the spring are followed by herb Bennet or wood avens with yellow five-petalled flowers, a member of the rose family. Two closely related plants are purple-flowered knapweeds: black knapweed is the smaller of the two with more compact flower-heads compared to greater knapweed with divided leaves and more spreading flower-heads. From May to July look among the leaves for female nurse spiders basking in the sun with their eight legs spread and held in four pairs. When the male is courting he catches an insect to present to the female as a gift before mating. He may carry it around for a day in his search, usually eating it himself if he is unsuccessful. The female carries her egg mass in her mouth until they are ready to hatch. She then forms a tent of leaves held by silk and places the eggs inside, standing guard over the young spiders, hence the name of nurse spider.

Where a gate crosses the track notice the line of the hedge linked by the gate. It marks the line of the boundary between Great Coxwell and Coleshill parishes and has followed this line for centuries. Trace its route across the fields; it is the only hedgeline which is not straight, showing how it follows the line of streams and old features in open fields, long since disappeared.

Continue along the track through the gate. An older landscape is still visible in the grassy ridges and furrows, the remains of the medieval ploughing system which left ridges of soil to keep the ground well drained. This group of ridge-and-furrow fields was part of Coleshill Field which was shared between villagers. It was still open field in 1761, although most of the rest of the parish was enclosed in 1451. This enclosure was unpopular with local people and there are records of hedgebreakers being fined. The formation shows particularly clearly when the sun is low in winter and in spring when the buttercups are in flower. Bulbous buttercups, identified by the down-turned green sepals underneath the flower and the swollen base to the stems, prefer drier ground and therefore tend to grow on the ridges. There are also many varied types of grasses growing here, most easily told apart when in flower. See how many you can spot.

Go through a second gateway and then at the third turn right through the farmyard.

Colleymore Farm was built at the time of the enclosure of the open field at the end of the eighteenth century. Swallows and martins fly about the yard during the summer, another example of how wildlife adapts to man-made habitats. The sides of the buildings make very suitable artificial cliff faces, the more usual nesting site for these species.

3 SU253941

At the main road cross straight over and continue down the track, turning right at the T-junction.

In the fairly recent past this now open track would have looked very different. Large stumps of elm trees killed by Dutch Elm disease would have given the landscape a much more wooded appearance. The slope on the right is Badbury Hill, the dark foliage of the conifers contrasting with the brighter green of the broad-leaved trees. In winter deciduous larch is obvious among the evergreen conifer species.

SHORT CUT *Turn right just before Brimstone Farm and follow the path across the fields and through the woods back to the car-park.*

At Brimstone Farm continue straight on through the yard and on to the next farm.

Look at the bright orange *Xanthoria* lichen on the roofs of the farm buildings. This attractive plant can be encouraged to colonize new roofs by spraying them with slurry to provide a nutrient rich base. This farm is older than Colleymore Farm passed earlier. It was shown on the Berkshire map of 1761, but the landscape ahead (north) was very different then. All this area is owned by the National Trust as part of the Buscot estate; Buscot Park was created towards the end of the eighteenth century from land that was previously arable and pasture. The next farm ahead of you is called Oldfield Farm, its name indicating the past landscape.

4 SU251261

At Oldfield Farm follow the path round the left-hand side of the farm, then turn right off the tarmac track onto a rough track towards a line of cottages.

Along the edge of this path are both red and white deadnettle, food sources for a variety of moths. As their name implies, these plants do not sting, in contrast to the quite unrelated stinging nettles to be seen near the cottages ahead, growing in disturbed ground rich in nutrients.

Bear right at the cottages and continue through a gate and over a small field. At the next gate turn sharp left along the field edge. As you walk along the field notice how every aspect of the landscape is in fact being quite intensively used by agriculture and forestry, with cereals, grass for silage and hay, fast-growing conifer trees for a quick investment and slower-growing deciduous trees for a long-term crop.

After following the field edge alongside Rowleaze Wood for a time, the path cuts across the corner of the field to a plank bridge over a ditch. Continue following the edge of Oak Wood for about half a mile (1 km).

Parts of this woodland are much older than the rest, the old woods now linked by modern planting. However, the boundaries of the original Eaton Wood and Coxwell Wood (now called Oak Wood) can be seen on the 1:25000 OS map, with possibly the outline of woodland felled centuries ago around the area of Wood House. Parts of the woodland show signs of traditional management. Coppicing (cutting to ground level) of hazel and ash produces multiple stems growing from one base, the practice being used in the past to produce supplies of small poles and wood for many everyday uses. In May the scent of bluebells fills the air. These well-known plants are the only widespread member of the lily family to be found wild in this country. They tend to be found in woodland where they will be undisturbed as they cannot withstand trampling or grazing although they will flourish in more open places.

Gorse

Horsetail

5   SU267955

At the end of the wood turn left and follow the track through a gateway and across the field. At the next gate take the stile on the right. Turn right along the bridleway, following the blue arrows across a large field. To the left is the landmark of Faringdon Folly on the hilltop which overlooks the town (see Walk 3).

Carry on through a gate and continue straight on, following the field edge on your left-hand side.

If the fields have been grazed by cattle you will notice dark green lush patches of grass. These mark where cow-pats have been, adding rich nutrients to the soil, so much in fact that the grass becomes too rich for the animals and they do not eat it. Cow-pats are used by a variety of insects as a place to lay their eggs before the surface dries out and becomes too hard. Yellow dung flies congregate quickly on fresh pats. The males arrive first and wait for the females which fly up wind to the pat where they are pounced on for mating by the waiting males. The male then rides on the female's back until she lays her eggs, and fights often occur as rival males try to take over a female and mate again.

Go through a gate, continue in the same direction to another gate, then uphill over grassland. Cross the gravel track then continue uphill to a small gate in the hedge.

As you climb up the slope look at changes in the vegetation on the left caused by a wet patch of ground. The bracken and gorse give way to plants such as marsh marigold, cuckoo flower, rushes, and marsh thistle with its purple spiny stems, all plants which like a damp habitat. There is a dense patch of horsetail, a primitive plant related to those which grew 300 million years ago in the subtropical swamps of the Carboniferous period. This is not a flowering plant, but forms spores at the end of a slender stem produced in May which is then replaced by the characteristic greenish stems bearing whorls of hard spiky 'leaves' which in the past were used for cleaning silver.

6 SU266948

At the top of the hill go through the small gate and turn right along a narrow road. After about 165 yards (150 m) turn left at a junction, over a stile and follow the path along a field edge bordered by woodland on the right.

The light conditions along the woodland edge encourage many wild flowers such as ground ivy, germander speedwell, primroses and dog's mercury. Look into the wood and you will see that the dense shade in the closely planted conifers eliminates flowering plants trying to grow beneath them.

The path enters the wood beside a group of larch trees which lose their leaves in winter and produce fresh green leaves in the spring. Feel the reduction in temperature and rise in humidity as you enter the wood from the

Sulphur-tuft toadstools

field. Dark brown and yellow speckled wood butterflies occur in the sunny patches, the males often using sunspots as courting territory. The woodland is quite mixed with cherry and crab-apple blossoming in the spring; other species include birch, oak, poplar, pine, larch and spruce. In autumn fungi can be seen in these woods, particular species often growing beneath specific trees. Large clusters of the aptly named sulphur-tuft toadstools are to be found on rotting tree stumps.

At a wide junction of paths turn left and go uphill back to the car-park.

The short cut rejoins at this point.

Passing through a yew grove it is interesting to note that recent evidence indicates that yews may reach a much greater age than previously supposed; some may be up to 2,000 years old, making them the oldest native trees in Britain.

As you approach the car-park compare the maple and sycamore trees along the path. Maples have longer teeth around the edge of the leaf and the flowers and seeds are in clusters, whereas sycamores have tassels hanging from a central stalk. Beech trees grow on the old Iron Age earthworks beside the car-park. Their fallen mast (fruit) provides good food for chaffinches and great tits as well as squirrels, mice and voles.

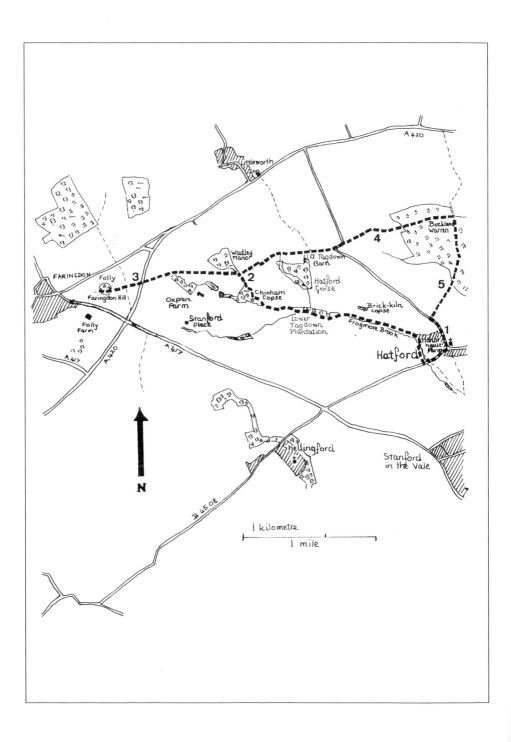

WALK 3

Hatford

7 miles   11.5 km

Short cut 5 miles 8 km

This mostly level walk leads through a quiet valley, with a diversion to the viewpoint of Faringdon Folly, reached by a short climb. Part of the return journey passes through an interesting and varied area of woodland. Some of the field walking may be muddy.

The diversion to Faringdon Folly starts from and returns to Point 2.

1 SU338948

Start in the village of Hatford in the lane close to Manorhouse Farm. On the main road, walk west out of the village towards Shellingford. The bank on the right-hand side of the road is home to a variety of plants. Many may be dwarfed because of the very well drained sandy soil, which gives rise to drought conditions. The deep blue flowers belong to wild clary, a fairly uncommon plant which belongs to the same family as sage. Both its common and Latin names (*Salvia horminoides*) indicate its use as a medicinal plant: Clary means 'clear eye' and salvia means 'healer'. It was used in the past as an eye ointment. Bright red poppies also grow here: the common poppy with a round seed-head and the long-headed poppy with a seed pod about twice as long as it is broad. These species are related to the

Hatford cottages

opium-producing poppy which has greyish stems and leaves and flowers ranging in colour from lilac to white. The interesting plants growing here have resulted in the County Council designating and managing this verge as a nature reserve.

Just over the bridge, climb the stile on the right and follow Frogmore Brook, keeping it on your right. Not quite 165 yards (150 m) further on, yellow arrows mark the route of the path as it crosses the stream and follows the bank, continuing through three gates and over a farm track.

Compare the vegetation on the banks of the stream with that of the grazed fields which contain few flowering herbs. Many of the waterside plants are good indicators of wet, marshy ground, and include hemp agrimony, meadowsweet, iris and sedge. The pale pink agrimony and the creamy-flowered meadowsweet are much used by insects as a source of nectar in the summer. Another plant seen here is dog's mercury, more usually found in woodland; its presence here may indicate a past woodland history. Closer to the water look for the dark green flat leaves of liverwort growing on the stony banks. These are very primitive plants whose ancestors originated in the Devonian geological period 350–400 million years ago. They need to be constantly moist and have very simple reproductive organs located in pits on the plant surface.

Although this valley is quiet now, there are indications of Romano-British settlement in the area, probably on the far side of the stream, built on the gravel terrace deposited by the stream. The small copse on the slope to the right was the site of a quarry where clay was extracted for brickmaking, probably in the nineteenth century, hence the name of Brick-kiln Copse.

The path passes to the right of a beech plantation which also contains lime trees. The many stems of the lime show that in the past they have been coppiced, although the thin shoots around the base of the trunks is characteristic of this species. There is another contrast in vegetation growing in different habitats. This time the plants in the woodland are those which like undisturbed conditions, like cowslips, dog's mercury and lords-and-ladies. The field edge is regularly ploughed and fertilized, and plants like stinging nettles, hogweed and hedge mustard can tolerate this. In early summer a large bright red and black day-flying moth may be seen here. This is the scarlet tiger moth which usually occurs in boggy areas. It has been the subject of considerable genetic and evolutionary studies for over fifty years in the Oxford area.

At a sharp right curve in the line of the stream, follow the path over a plank bridge (the second to be seen) and into the woodland. The path follows the left-hand woodland edge.

The sheltered conditions of the wood, which was probably planted at the beginning of the nineteenth century, provides homes for many birds and animals. Wrens, robins, chaffinches, blue and great tits can all be seen and heard in the wood, as can the summer migrant chiff-chaff, easily identified as it calls its

Louise V. Spicer

Scarlet tiger moths

name. Foxes may be seen here. The earth, an underground burrow, is usually taken over from badgers or rabbits. Evidence of squirrels, mice and voles can also be found. Hazelnut shells on the ground will be split in half by squirrels but mice and voles gnaw at the shells to make distinctive holes. In soft mud you may also spot the two-toed footprints of deer. All these signs demonstrate the value of woodland in the agricultural landscape as a source of food and shelter for wildlife.

Insects too make their homes here. On bright sunny days in summer, look out for male hover-flies using sunny spots as courtship territories. Many hover-flies are patterned in black and yellow, and mimic bees and wasps to fool their predators that these harmless flies are actually stinging insects. Brown speckled wood butterflies also court and bask in the sun spots, and their caterpillars feed on some of the grasses growing in the woodland. The sycamore trees support huge numbers of sycamore aphids which are very important food sources for several birds. These aphids do not like close company, so space themselves evenly on the underside of the leaves. If disturbed they produce an 'alarm' odour to warn their neighbours, causing a cloud of insects to fly off the leaf together. Sycamore is thought to have been introduced into this country probably in the fifteenth or sixteenth centuries. It seeds prolifically and for this reason is often disliked as it tends to crowd out the original trees in a woodland. Several types of gill fungi may be found in this woodland, especially in autumn. They can be distinguished by the variable shapes and colours of their caps.

The path emerges from the wood, but after a few metres takes another track once more through the woodland. On eventually leaving the wood, follow the field edge which soon becomes a wide grassy track with a hedge on the left.

Chinham Copse ahead contains varied tree species, shown by the different colours through the year. In spring the blackthorn bushes are covered with white flowers before the leaves burst, while the silvery leaves of white poplar contrast with the darker green of sycamore and oak. Oak often has a reddish tinge in August when new shoots called Lammas growth appear in a bid to outwit the many insects which feed on oak. Poplar produces masses of white fluffy seeds in late summer and its leaves are some of the first to change colour and fall in the autumn. Along the path is a substantial black poplar with less hairy leaves shaped like the ace of spades. The tall arching branches were used in the past as cruck beams in building, the natural shape being ideal for supports.

As the path bends round look back along the valley for a good view across the fields to Didcot Power Station with the Downs behind.

2   SU313958

When the path reaches a junction, either turn right for a shorter walk, or for a diversion to Faringdon Folly

Sand-martin at nest

on the hilltop, take the white stile on the left and cross diagonally over the field to a track.

Diversion to Faringdon Folly

If you look to the left you will see a large pond some distance away. Sand-martins can be seen in summer swooping over the water to catch flies and other

Canada geese

insects. They are easily distinguished from swallows by the blunt forked tail and from house-martins by the brown coloration. They may be nesting in the sandy banks bordering the pond or in sand cliffs nearby.

This open water has provided an alternative site to the River Thames for a variety of waterfowl including moorhens (with red bills), coots (with white head patches), and mallard. Canada geese were introduced from North America in the nineteenth century and have escaped from ornamental lakes to spread throughout the Thames valley and other lowland water sites. They are becoming a nuisance because of the damage they cause in grazing fields and open spaces.

Cross the track, go over another stile and follow the path straight ahead across the field to the white stile in the left corner of the field. Follow the field edge to a wooden stile on to the A420.

3 SU302957

Cross the busy Faringdon bypass with care and climb

Faringdon Folly

the stile opposite. Follow the path uphill across the field and over another stile. Continue straight on to the top of the hill.

The soil here is again sandy. This type of soil does not retain water so plants often have to live under near drought conditions. Many growing here are members of the pea family – white clover, common meddick and common vetch. They can supplement their nutrients from the soil by 'fixing' nitrogen from the air with the help of special bacteria living in nodules on their roots. Scots pines are planted at the top of the hill; they like acid soil and can be recognized by their orange bark and short needles growing in pairs. The pines were originally planted in 1790 by Henry James Pye, the then Poet Laureate, and were regarded as a folly. Many have since been replaced.

The most obvious landmark on the hilltop is the tower, built in 1935 by Lord Berner as a modern folly. However, in earlier times this strategic hill was used for more serious purposes. There was a Cromwellian

Field pansy

gun battery here during the Civil War using the remains of a medieval castle motte (mound).

The view from this vantage point is extensive and it is said that six counties can be seen. The history of the area is laid out in the landscape, including ancient geological marine deposits of sand and gravel now being extracted, the Iron Age White Horse on the Downs to the south, the town of Faringdon dating back to before the Norman conquest, regular-shaped eighteenth and nineteenth-century enclosure fields with straight hedges, new and old roads reflecting changes in importance of towns, Brize Norton airfield, Didcot Power Station and changing crops with yellow rape seed often taking the place of the softer colours of the cereal crops.

Retrace your steps downhill and return to Point 2. Once over the white stile turn left and follow the bridleway.

End of diversion

All along the wide path are numerous wild flowers including white campion, poppy, and mignonette with its tall spikes of pale yellow flowers much liked by bees. Another plant with small yellow flowers is the field pansy. This favours open disturbed ground unlike the related violets which are found only in woodland and undisturbed hedgerows. You may also find the wild pansy which has slightly larger purple and yellow flowers. Notice how all these species produce plants of varying sizes, unlike cultivated garden species with very similar sized individuals. Wild plants are much more tolerant of varying conditions and can produce flowers and seed on large or small plants. On the grass verge in autumn you may find shaggy ink cap fungi, so called because their black spores are released by the liquefaction of the gills, dissolving into a black ink-like secretion within a few hours. The caps also resemble barristers' wigs, hence the other name of Lawyer's Wig.

Wild pansy

The trail continues through large open fields where you may see brown hares and on past Tagdown Barn.

57

Tagdown Barn

These are solitary animals which live in 'forms' or slight depressions in the ground, unlike rabbits in their social burrows. Hares rely on their swiftness to escape their main predator, the fox. The path follows the same route as one shown on the 1761 map. However, this is now no more than a farm track whereas many other such routes have been tarred and today are roads.

When the road is reached turn left for a short distance then take the bridleway off on the right to continue in the same direction as before. The bridleway leads to a thick hedge which marks the boundary between Hatford and Buckland parishes. The stag head oak may also have acted as a marker in the past.

Continue on through a golf course, the way being fenced by metal railings.

4 SU333963

Soon the path reaches woodland. A notice requests dogs to be kept on leads. Follow the path for about half a mile (1 km) until a junction is reached close to a field. Turn right here for a further half a mile.

The history of this woodland is sketchy but on the Rocque map of Berkshire of 1761 this area was shown as commonland in the parish of Buckland. An earlier survey of the estate of Sir John Yate of Buckland made in 1648 records a coney (rabbit) warren in this area, rabbits then being kept in enclosed warrens to provide meat. This area is still named Buckland Warren on the Ordnance Survey map. However, by about 1830 most of the present-day woodland had been planted and was called Buckland Cover.

The many unusual and ornamental species present in the woodland point to its fairly recent origin. Look for Corsican pine which is similar to Scots pine except that the bark is grey instead of orange and the needles and cones are larger. Evergreen or holm oak is another continental introduction and unlike the native oaks keeps its leaves all year. Rhododendron is an introduction from Asia and has spectacular flowers in late spring. It was originally often planted as game cover, as it probably was here. In many parts of the country it has become a serious pest as it has spread and formed impenetrable thickets, shading out ground plants, so that active steps have to be taken to control it. The young growing shoots are protected by a very sticky secretion, trapping insects which die in the glue. Another exotic tree is the monkey puzzle with most of its branches near the top of the trunk. The leaves are scale-like with needle-like tips, growing all round the shoot, and the large round cones can grow as big as footballs.

In the sandy soil along the edge of the path look out for a small white-flowered plant growing in large clumps. This is spring beauty; the top pair of leaves form a cup around the flower-bearing stem. This is yet another introduced plant, this time from North America, which likes acid sandy soil.

After the right turn the path eventually passes through a yew grove. The yew, Scots pine and juniper are Britain's only native conifers. Yew tolerates heavy shade and can grow beneath the canopy of other trees. Birds like the pink flesh around the seeds but the seed itself and the leaves are poisonous.

Close to the edge of the woodland notice how some of the smaller oak trees bear various types of galls. Large irregular-shaped whitish galls are oak apples, the smaller very round brown galls are oak marbles and, underneath some leaves, are flattened spangle galls. These are all caused by different types of tiny wasps laying eggs on the developing buds or leaves. The growing larva stimulates the tree to produce a 'cancerous' growth inside which it lives for protection. A small hole in a gall shows where the adult wasp has emerged.

5 SU339956

The path emerges into fields again. Look back and see the outline of the wood which follows the line of the parish boundary seen earlier. This ex-commonland is typically placed at the edge of a parish where the sandy soil would have provided only marginal cultivation.

Follow the path across the field towards the road.

On the right a sand extraction site again reflects the impact of human activity in shaping the landscape.

Hop flowers

Evidence of Iron Age habitation has been found here showing how land use is never static.

At the road turn left and return to Hatford and the starting point.

The verges are rich in wild flowers. Look for the entwining stems of hop trailing over the hedge to the left. It is interesting to note that this plant is related to elm and to stinging nettles. Insects like the comma butterfly recognize this botanical similarity in these very different looking plants and lay their eggs on all of them. In years to come the appearance of this lane will slowly change as the planted lime, ash and cherry trees grow up and dominate the view.

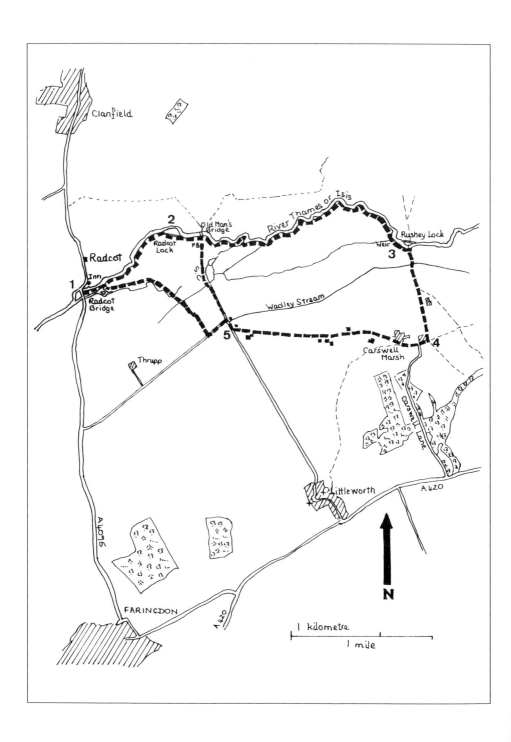

Radcot Bridge

7.5 miles   9 km

Short cut 3 miles 5 km

Including one of the oldest bridges on the Thames, this walk follows the line of the river, then returns through quiet countryside. Some field edges may be muddy in wet weather.

A short cut can be taken to reduce the length of the walk.

1   SU285995

Car parking is limited in this area so either start from Radcot Bridge or from other points along the trail.

Starting from Radcot Bridge, take the path over the grass beside the river, heading downstream to a wooden bridge.

Radcot is the site of one of the oldest river crossings of the Thames. There was a simple stone bridge here by AD 958, mentioned in a charter which described the boundaries of the Manor of Longworth. The two present bridges are many centuries apart in age. The medieval bridge has three arches and is thought to have been constructed during the thirteenth century. The centre arch was rebuilt towards the end of the fourteenth century, following damage during the Battle of Radcot between supporters of Henry of Lancaster

Radcot Bridge

and Richard II. Much of the original stonework remains standing on the original timber raft foundations. Although narrow by today's standards, the bridge was wide enough for two laden pack-horses to pass, this being a main route for the transport of wool from the Cotswolds to London. During the Civil War, Radcot Bridge was a key point for the defence of Oxford, but thereafter the bridge declined in importance until the opening of the Thames & Severn Canal. A survey made in 1787 found the bridge to be too narrow to allow the passage of laden barges, so it was decided to construct a new channel for navigation purposes with a new bridge, which is the one nearest the pub. The channel and bridge were completed by 1789 at a cost of almost £400. The widest channel of the river today is therefore the two-hundred-year-old cut.

There was a river port here even before the Norman Conquest when Berkshire cheese was taken down river. Later, it was a centre for the transport of stone quarried in the Cotswolds at Taynton and Burford which was used for building the colleges in Oxford,

Coot on nest

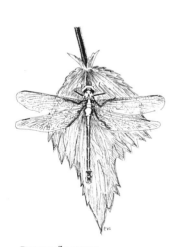

Dragon-fly at rest

and St Paul's and other buildings in London. Now the smart pleasure craft along the river reflect a very different connection with the waterway compared with the working barges of the past.

Pause on the wooden foot-bridge for a few moments.

The less busy waterway has reeds and rushes growing along its banks which are used by coots and moorhens as material for their substantial but often well hidden nests. Both birds feed on submerged vegetation which they collect by diving. Dragon-flies and smaller slender-bodied damselflies live here, those in the deep flowing river requiring different conditions to those in ditches and still water.

Go through the gates on the bridge, then turn left and follow the riverbank for about 3 miles (5 km).

As you walk notice the fields across the river. Rows of willow have been planted which will be used for cricket-bat wood, about seven bats being made from each tree. Willow grows very easily from sticks put in the ground and represents a good example of an alternative agricultural crop.

Along this first stretch of the river look out for two plants which are only found close to water. Celery-leaved buttercup has clusters of small yellow flowers and only grows where the muddy ground is disturbed by trampling to provide the conditions needed for seed germination. Gypsywort has white flowers and toothed leaves and is related to mint and thyme although this plant is not aromatic. However, it produces a dark coloured dye which it is said was used by gypsies to darken their skin.

Celery-leaved buttercup

In places the riverbank is exposed, revealing the layer of alluvial soil overlying a bed of gravel, both deposited by the action of the river. In many places along the river it is obvious how the banks provide a wildlife refuge for many plants and associated animals that are absent from the cultivated fields. Some plants prefer the wet conditions, but others escape grazing and grow here. Occasional drinking places show how cattle trample and graze the vegetation.

2   SP296002

Continue alongside the river, through a double gate and, further along, over a stile to Radcot Lock.

This lock and weir date from the 1890s when the old flash lock a little further downstream was superseded. This was called Old Man's Weir and the site is now marked by a foot-bridge. The site of another flash lock, Old Nan's Weir has now disappeared completely.

In contrast to the grazed fields crossed earlier, here the verge along the path is rich in flowers. Plants often growing in wet ground such as meadowsweet, comfrey and yellow flag are mixed with white deadnettle, spear thistle, ground ivy and cut-leaved geranium. Just past the lock on the far bank is a clump of broad-leaved great water dock. This was the food plant for the larvae of the large copper butterfly which became extinct in Britain at the end of the nineteenth century due to the

Gypsywort

draining of its wetland habitat and over collection by specimen hunters. Although efforts have been made to re-introduce the butterfly in East Anglia, an enormous amount of effort and money is needed to reinstate and manage the correct habitat. In contrast the small copper butterfly is common throughout Britain as its caterpillars feed on a variety of docks and sorrels.

The path continues along the river past the foot-bridge at Old Man's Bridge and on downstream.

SHORT CUT *At Old Man's Bridge go over the cattle-grid and turn right. Follow the path along the hedgeline and along a track to rejoin the walk at Point 5.*

The fields past the foot-bridge are colourful with buttercups in the spring and early summer. See if you can identify three different species. Creeping buttercup has smooth flower stalks in contrast to bulbous buttercup with furrowed flower stalks and turned down

Goldfinch on teasel

sepals beneath the petals. Meadow buttercup is a taller, more delicate plant, also with smooth stalks, but with more divided leaves than the creeping buttercup. Even if the fields are grazed, buttercups tend to survive as they irritate the mouths of cattle causing blisters.

The concrete structure across the river is a pillbox, built in the Second World War as part of a defensive line when German invasion threatened.

For a short distance the path passes through a group of crack willows. These trees are more usually seen

House-martin (upper), swallow (middle), swift (lower)

pollarded – cut back at head height – but these have been left to grow naturally. Large branches break under their own weight and often tear open the trunk. Old wood may rot away leaving hollow trunks which may be colonized by dogroses or hawthorn.

In the second half of the year, the stiff, dead seed-heads of thistles, teasels and figwort attract groups or 'charms' of goldfinches. These colourful finches with scarlet faces and black and yellow wings cling adroitly to the plants, extracting the seeds with their short strong bills. Swallows and martins can be seen flying over the water in summer catching insects. The swift, a similar bird, may also be present. Although not related to the others it has even more refined flying capabilities and can stay airborne for long periods, even sleeping on the wing. It is one of the last spring migrants to arrive and the first to leave for its winter home in southern Africa. In winter flocks of lapwings frequent the nearby fields. Their slow flapping flight

Lapwing

gives them their name and their distinctive call provides the alternative title of pee-wit. This species has been depleted due to loss of breeding habitat. However, they should be encouraged as they eat many pests such as leather-jackets and wire-worms. Another bird with an evocative call, occasionally seen in this area, is the curlew. This is a large wader, easily recognized by its very long, down-curved bill.

3 SP322001

Go through a gate and over a foot-bridge.

A small wet cutting contains tall Phragmites reeds. These are the once important thatching reeds and the thick clumps are home to such birds as reed-buntings; the singing males with brown backs and black heads may be seen chirring from the tops of tall reed stems.

At Rushey lock go past the weir and follow the path over a stile.

Rushey Lock was one of the first to be modernized with the coming of the Thames & Severn Canal, and

Rushey Lock

was built in 1790 when there was a toll of $2\frac{1}{2}d$ (1p). Now it is one of the few remaining paddle weirs on the Thames, operated by a system of paddles placed against wooden posts or rymers to control the head of water above the weir. This point is likely to have been used as a crossing during the Middle Ages, and there was a ferry here in the early nineteenth century.

Look out for the path turning off to the right about 55 yards (50 m) further on which may be hidden in lush grass. Go over a bank, down a dip and through a group of trees. Continue along a well-defined field path with the hedge on your right for just over half a mile (1 km) until some cottages are reached.

Notice the trees in the hedge alongside the path. They are introduced turkey oaks with dark narrow leaves and bristly acorn cups. Along the field edge notice examples of 'weeds of cultivation' which were absent in the grazed fields along the riverbank. It is interesting to realize that these species took advantage of early man's agricultural efforts instead of having to rely on naturally disturbed soil for a habitat.

White bryony

Evidence of their presence has been found in pollen preserved in peat bogs; this gives a picture of the flora of Britain since the last Ice Age and shows that cultivation first occurred in the Neolithic period around 4,000 years ago. A climbing plant in the hedgerow is white bryony with tendrils which grip any convenient support. The tendril stems are sensitive to contact and once they touch something the stems curve towards it, curling round the touched object. The yellowish flowers produce orange-red berries which are very poisonous.

The hills ahead are part of the ridge of Corallian limestone which stretches from Oxford to Faringdon (see Introduction).

4   SU326989

When you reach a group of cottages, turn right following the blue bridleway signs. Go past the cottages, then straight on along Carswell farm track, ignoring Carswell Lane on the left leading uphill.

This area is called Carswell Marsh and these cottages and farms appear to be little altered since they were shown on the 1761 map. There is evidence of medieval agriculture in the ridge-and-furrow fields alongside the track, which appears to have been more important in the past.

Along the track, low-growing but conspicuous clumps of delicate spiky leaves with feathery yellow flower-heads in midsummer are Lady's bedstraw. The name refers to the legend that the plant was included in the bedding straw at the Nativity, 'Lady' referring to the Virgin Mary. Other plants such as Lady's mantle, Lady's smock and Lady's slipper all have similar connotations.

Follow the track, ignoring the footpath which goes off to the left. About 55 yards (50 m) past Carswell Farm look for a bridleway sign beside a stile and follow this line diagonally left across the field. You will reach a foot-bridge beside a dried-up pond. Go through the gate and continue over the next field to a metal gate and bridge. Follow the footpath through the garden and then through the large gate and down the track through another field which shows signs of ridge-and-furrow. Continue straight on along this track for just over half a mile (1 km).

This narrow tarmac path is bordered by mixed hedges on each side. In spring there is a profusion of blossom. The earliest is blackthorn or sloe whose flowers appear before the leaves. Hawthorn flowers after the leaves have burst, often in May as its alternative name implies. Later come field maple, buckthorn, dogrose, and bramble. The flowers and leaves are good food sources for insects, and the autumn berries add more colour to the hedgerow as well as providing food for birds, mice and voles.

5   SU302990

The track emerges onto the road which leads to Littleworth. Turn right along the road and follow it round the right-angled bend to the left.

The short cut rejoins here. Turn right when you reach the road.

The area towards Littleworth on the hill behind was commonland until the nineteenth century, as was the area through which you are about to walk. This was Thrupp Common in the 1830s but on the 1761 map was called Pond Common. There is no sign of the common now except for the quite wide road verges which were often left when commonland was enclosed and existing tracks improved or new roads laid out.

A little further along take the path off to the right along the field edge, keeping the hedge on your left.

Half-way down the field the path crosses to the other side of the ditch; continue in the same direction as before.

The hawthorn hedge was probably planted when the common was enclosed but a line of oaks and field maples has recently been planted which will grow up to give more variety to the landscape as well as additional habitats for birds and insects.

Ahead, a line of large crack willows marks the course of a small stream. There are many different types of willow in this country. Many of them are very similar to one another and are very difficult to identify. The crack willow belongs to a group of long-leaved species and nearby are some goat willows belonging to a round-leaved group. These bear the well known pussy-willow catkins on the male trees, an important source of food in early spring for bumble-bees and butterflies like the comma when it comes out of hibernation. The female catkins are green and spiky, producing fluffy white cotton down seeds which blow about in the wind in late spring.

At the stream, go over two water-filled ditches, through a gate and over a stile, then straight on along

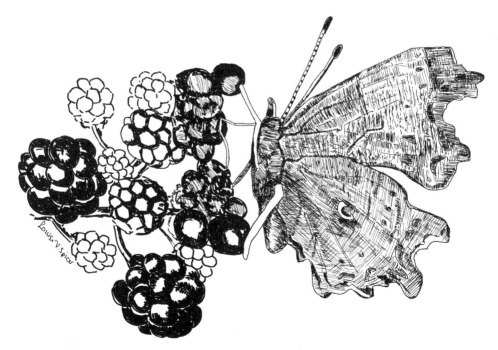

Comma butterfly feeding on blackberry

the hedgeline as before. At the end of the field, go through a small gate on the left then right through a narrow passageway over a foot-bridge and stile into a narrow field. Follow the left hedgeline as the field opens out, then cross the field to reach the wooden foot-bridge within sight of Radcot Bridge and the starting place.

This large field may be sheep grazed. Notice how narrow paths have been made by the sheep walking in single file, an instinct remaining from their mountain ancestry. In contrast, most people tend to walk in a wide group which in sensitive areas can lead to bad footpath erosion.

Just across the field on the left, situated on the old river channel, was a weir with a mill which dated back to before 1429. It appears on the 1761 map where it is called Monks Mill, perhaps a link with the Cistercian monks who owned land in the Faringdon area (see Walk 2).

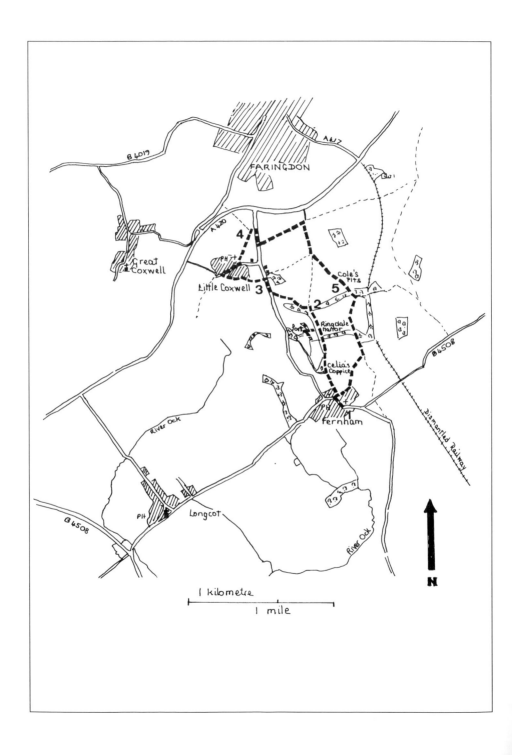

FARINGDON

B 4019

A 417

A 420

Great
Coxwell

PH +

Little Coxwell

Cole's
Pits

4

3

2

5

Ringdale
Manor

Celia's
Coppice

1

Fernham

River Ock

B 4508

Dismantled Railway

River Ock

B 4508

Pit

Longcot

N

1 kilometre

1 mile

Fernham

3.5 miles   5.5 km

This route leads to the old village of Little Coxwell and through varied scenery with good views over the Vale of the White Horse. It can be muddy in places.

1   SU294918

Start opposite the church near a trough and pump, heading left uphill towards Faringdon.

The church is relatively modern, built in the middle of the nineteenth century by the brother of Thomas Hughes, the author of *Tom Brown's Schooldays*, who lived nearby at Uffington. Several plants make their homes in the wall surrounding the churchyard. Look for a plant with creeping stems, distinctive-shaped leaves and flowers like small snapdragons. This is ivy-leaved toadflax, a plant which came originally from southern Europe. The flower stalks rise above the leaves and project away from the wall. However, when the seeds are developing, the stem curls backwards to the wall and grows into crevices and ledges so that the seeds are shed into the wall rather than falling onto the ground. Plants which grow on walls tend to be rather specialized, able to tolerate the lime in the mortar and the low nutrients in the sparse soil, and are resistant to desiccation.

On the left beside a cottage is a large box tree with small oval evergreen leaves. This slow-growing shrub

Village water pump

Ivy-leaved toadflax

is often used for hedging and topiary, the bushes being clipped into exotic shapes. Its yellow wood is very hard and dense, and has been used for centuries for carving and inlays. Another use was for wood engravings such as those produced by Thomas Bewick.

Turn right into Chapel Lane walking past a box hedge on your right. Take the footpath signposted to Faringdon on the left, cross the stile and walk uphill along the right-hand field edge to another stile. Continue along the path at the edge of a copse.

This is now called Celia's Coppice but in the past the hill was unwooded and known as Furze Hill, furze being another name for gorse. The origins of both plant names indicate much about the past use of this shrub. Gorse comes from an Anglo-Saxon word meaning a 'waste', gorse often growing in rough places not suitable for agriculture because of poor soil.

79

Furze originates from another Anglo-Saxon word 'fyrs' or firewood. The shrub was widely used for fuel, especially in places with little woodland. It is interesting to see further on along the path that plenty of gorse still grows here on the sandy soil and that on the 1761 map at least part of this hill was commonland or 'waste'.

Sycamore grows in the copse. In summer the leaves may have penny-sized black spots on them. These are infected by a fungus appropriately called the tar-spot fungus. The leaf points on sycamore are rather short and blunt compared to the longer and more tapered ones on maple which you will encounter a little further along the trail. The fallen leaves in autumn are quite dull in colour compared to the rich colours of other members of the maple family. The copse is

Toadstool

Puff-balls

useful cover for game birds such as pheasants and partridges which you may see in the fields nearby. These need the woodland for protection but will feed in the open fields as well. Tall grassy vegetation can be hazardous for very young birds, as rain and dew will wet them thoroughly and they may die of cold in bad weather.

As you walk along the path look at the view of the Ock valley spreading out on the right. In the far distance are the Downs with the White Horse Iron Age chalk carving and the valley below it, known as the Manger. Further away are the cooling towers of Didcot Power Station and, on a clear day, the line of the Chiltern Hills should be visible beyond (see Book 2, *Chilterns*). Closer, notice the fields just below you. They are good examples of ridge-and-furrow, preserved from the time that old open fields were grassed over for pasture land and not ploughed since.

As the path enters a conifer plantation, look out for the hedgebank on the right. It is topped by coppiced hazel, very obvious in winter, which forms a thick barrier of growth. The younger twigs have hairy stems, making this plant easy to identify even in winter before the appearance of the familiar yellow catkins. The field edge alongside the hazel may be planted with a narrow belt of kale or other crop left to over-winter. This gives food and cover for game birds and is a feature frequently seen in field corners or edges. Many of the conifers here are larch which shed their leaves in winter. They turn bright yellow in autumn and in spring the new leaves are a bright fresh green, which contrast well with the dark colours of the other evergreens. The young female cones are dark magenta, quite distinct from the clusters of very small pollen-bearing male cones.

In autumn, several different types of fungi may be found along this part of the walk. The descriptively named lawyer's wigs or shaggy ink caps grow on the grassy verge, while under the trees look for clusters or rings of white funnel-shaped toadstools and pale yellow puff-balls.

2 SU295931

Continue straight on and just past the house look left across the field. The mounds and ditches are the remnants of an Iron Age hill fort with a circular bank enclosing almost twelve acres. This is one of many in the area but there are differing views as to the uses for the 'forts'. Some see them as defensive positions while others think of them as settlements and market places. Whatever their purpose, there was obviously a large population in this part of the upper Thames valley in the centuries prior to the Roman invasion.

At the next junction through the trees, turn left.

There is quite a variety of trees planted here. Scots pine can be recognized by its orange bark, especially obvious towards the top of the trunk. Cypress has dense foliage with very small scale-like leaves closely pressed to the stems. The cones are eaten by squirrels and the stripped stems can be found on the ground. Both maple and sycamore grow here; see if you can recognize the leaf difference mentioned earlier. They seed prolifically and dense patches of seedlings occur in some places, many of which will be eaten by slugs, snails and small animals.

There is a large rabbit warren on the hedgebank on the right. Rabbits were introduced to this country probably by the Normans and for centuries were kept in artificial warrens as they were too delicate to live without help in this country. However, over the centuries they adapted and escaped until they became widespread and regarded as a pest.

On the hill to the left more of the Iron Age fort can be seen. The hillside shows some remnants of the commonland which remained in use here in the parish of Little Coxwell until about 1801. Yellow-flowered gorse is likely to be visible throughout the year as it is capable of self pollination. It has been suggested that winter flowering is a means to escape predation by a beetle which lays its eggs on the soft developing seed-pod. The larva then eats the seeds inside, maturing into the adult beetle which can only escape when the pod bursts open. If the plants produce some flowers in the winter these seeds may survive as the beetle is not active then. Whatever the reason, the bright splash of colour is always welcome.

3   SU285931

At the road turn right towards Little Coxwell, then take the path which goes off to the left about 220 yards (200 m) along the road.

The fields on the left along the road were originally more commonland called Cow Common but were made into agricultural land in 1801 when Little Coxwell was enclosed. The parallel straight hedges bounding the fields are characteristic enclosure hedges. The road was probably defined at the same time and is a typical straight enclosure road with wide verges.

Over the stile, follow the path across two fields and past a pond.

These fields have a different history to the ones further back along the road. Traces of ridge-and-

Little Coxwell cottages

furrow show that they were used for arable land before being grassed over for grazing. There are likely to be geese by the pond. Domestic geese are probably derived from the wild greylag goose; they are quite aggressive and noisy. In the past geese were kept to graze on commonland by poor people who could use their eggs, meat, feathers and down. Farm and village ponds were a common sight in the past but many have been filled in or have dried out. Those remaining are invaluable wildlife habitats.

Continue on between the wall and the tennis court, following the line of the wall to a wooden gate beside a row of stables.

The young trees in the field are limes, another species which harbours large numbers of aphids in summer. They feed on the sugar-rich sap and excrete large amounts of excess sugar which forms a shiny coating on the leaves (and parked cars) in dry weather. As summer advances a dark fungus starts to grow on the sugar making the leaves look dirty but in heavy rain this is washed off. Ladybirds and hover-flies often lay their eggs on lime trees where the larvae feed on the aphids.

Turn right along the track to the road where you turn right into Little Coxwell.

Walking through the village, notice the old water-pump outside the pub. This would have been the only water supply for the villagers until relatively recently. The layout of the village is little altered from that of two hundred years ago. The sunken road shows the years of use before it was given a hard surface.

Continue straight on until you reach a footpath to the left at the end of the row of cottages which leads to the church. The church dates from the twelfth century and is worth a visit.

Past the church follow the path which goes right along the field edge next to a wall and then in the same direction across the next field. On the map of 1761 this area was called Coxwell Fields. It was probably used as arable open fields up to the enclosures in 1801, in contrast to the ridge-and-furrow fields passed earlier which were likely to have been enclosed much earlier, so preserving the furrows. The cultivated grassland contains few flowers especially if the fields are heavily grazed. The only plants to survive are those which are protected like bitter tasting docks or prickly, hard-to-eat thistles and nettles.

4   SU284939

Climb a stile and turn right for a few yards. At the road turn right for about 220 yards (200 m), then turn left along a bridleway.

Elm is a conspicuous species in the roadside hedge. Although Dutch Elm disease killed many big trees, these hedge trees have been able to survive because new suckers are produced from old roots which thus produce a good, thick hedge. The leaves can be identified by the tough sandpapery texture.

This bridleway was more important in the past. Interestingly, it follows a more or less parallel route to the present-day Faringdon bypass, opened in 1979, possibly a function of this track in the past.

After a time the track is hedged on both sides and a

junction is reached. Turn right here up the track which again in the past was used more than now.

This is a good place to notice the soil and how it changes along the walk. Much of the ground is sandy, and not far from the junction to the left there is a gravel quarry, reflecting the past geological history of this area when it was part of an inland sea and these deposits were laid down. You may also be lucky enough to find fossils on the path which becomes more stony as it climbs up the ridge of Corallian limestone forming the line of hills around Faringdon (see Introduction).

Ignore the footpath sign and continue along the track.

Another feature which has now sadly disappeared was a site known as Cole's Pits on the left at the top of the hill. These pits were medieval quarries from which stone for millstones and hand-operated querns or mills was obtained. There were over two hundred pits and in the 1930s some were measured and found to be over 30 feet (10 m deep). The name dates back to at least the seventeenth century, although John Rocque the 1761 map-maker just labels the area as 'A Pitt'. There are good views from this point. Great Coxwell Barn can be seen over to the right (Walk 2) and White Horse Hill is ahead.

This path is full of calcium-loving plants like scabious with delicate mauve flowers and knapweed with bulkier purple flowers. Poppies and mignonette provide food for bees and other insects, while meadow-brown and marbled-white butterflies occur here, their caterpillars feeding on grasses. Large clumps of mugwort can also be found, a plant which repels rather than attracts insects. In the past the crushed leaves were used in houses to get rid of fleas. The tall grass along the track is false-oat grass, so called because of its similarity to oats. However, the seeds are easily dropped when ripe if you run your finger along the seed-head. This feature common to wild grasses would be no use for cultivated cereals as they would be impossible to harvest. Ancient farmers gradually selected plants in which seeds were difficult to dislodge, hence the need for threshing to remove the grain from the husk.

5   SU295932

The track goes downhill to a junction. Bear left into the trees. Turn right soon after and follow the path uphill. Continue on this track for some distance.

In the copse look out for field maple which has similar but much smaller leaves to sycamore and maple. Unlike these introduced species, field maple is native to this country. Its leaves often bear hundreds of small warts, which are galls produced by tiny leaf-burrowing mites related to similar ones on lime and elm leaves. Silver birch has been planted here and the summer catkins are female containing hundreds of small seeds tightly stacked like plates. The male catkins are produced in spring and fall off once the pollen is shed. The seeds are very light and can float long distances so making this tree a good colonizing species and often the first to be found on waste ground.

When the track leaves the woodland, after about 220 yards (200 m), look out for a path through a gate on the right. Follow the path diagonally across the field to another gate at the right of the farm and go on to the stile. Head down the quiet road then left onto the main road and back to the start.

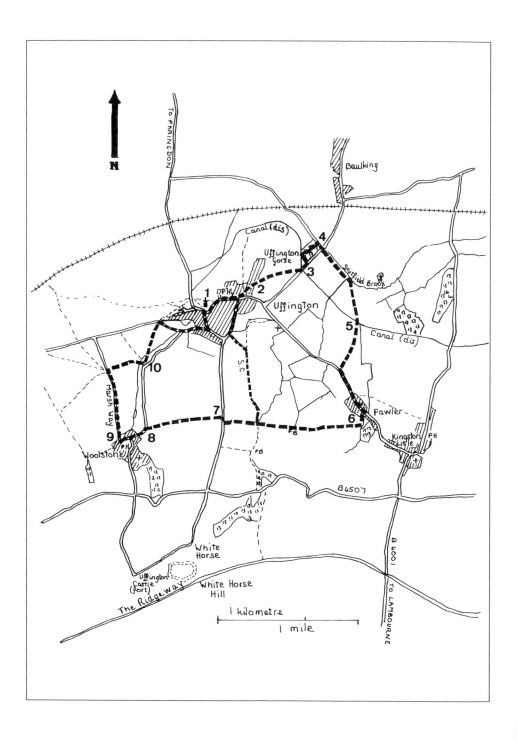

Uffington

5.5 miles   9 km

Short cut 4 miles 6.5 km

This level walk lies under the escarpment of the Downs, with the famous White Horse visible from much of the route. A short cut can reduce the distance of the walk.

1   SU303894

In Uffington, start from the main street, going past St Mary's church, the village school and the White Horse pub in that order. Continue to a road junction opposite an open expanse of grass.

Uffington belonged to the Abbey of Abingdon, granted by Aethelstan in AD 927. St Mary's church was built in the first part of the thirteenth century, possibly on the site of an earlier building. Known as the Cathedral of the Vale, the church used to have a spire until it was destroyed in a storm in December 1740. Many of the old village buildings are of chalk ashlar (dressed stone), contrasting with the modern brick-built bungalows and houses. The older houses tend to be built close to the road whereas the newer buildings are set back with front gardens.

At the junction, take the tarred footpath on the left, opposite the High Street. Continue straight on at the

St Mary's church, Uffington

next two junctions until you reach the last of the houses.

Along the path, look at the hawthorn hedge. In early summer the new shoots will be covered in frothy 'cuckoo-spit'. The young stages of froghopper insects feed on the sap of the plant and excrete lots of water as they feed. They blow bubbles into the water, so producing foam which acts as a protection against enemies.

2 SU308896

Just past the last house, take the path on the right which leads diagonally left to the far corner of the field. Cross the track and continue in the same direction as before to reach a stile leading onto the road.

These fields were once part of Uffington Common which was enclosed in 1778. The bumps in the first field may date from this time, possibly indicating where people had rights to dig up clay or other useful minerals. Another possibility is that they mark the line of a now-disappeared watercourse.

The fields may be grazed by cattle; the grassland has been improved by fertilizer and contains fewer wild flowers than the nearby hedgerows as the vigorous grasses outgrow them. Thistles, nettles and ducks often become problems in grazing fields as the prickly, irritating or bitter leaves are not eaten by the animals. Dark green lush grass indicates where a cow-pat has enriched the soil, encouraging the grass to grow. However, this grass is too rich for the animals to eat and they tend to leave it alone. Thus it is important for farmers to break up cow-pats in fields to reduce the growth of these clumps of enriched grass.

Nettle patches often develop large populations of nettle aphids. Small two-spot ladybirds often feed on these serving an important pest control function. Normally these beetles are red with two black spots, hence the name, but sometimes you may find a different type which is black with red spots. This is called the melanic (i.e. black) form and is more frequent in polluted city areas but also regularly occurs in parts of the country with cool, moist weather. It is said that the dark colour helps the insect to absorb heat which helps it stay active when conditions are cool.

3 SU313898

On the road turn left, then after 220 yards (200 m) left again over a stile into woodland.

A slight rise in the road as it passes the edge of the woodland and an overgrown hollow alongside the road are all that remains here of the Wiltshire & Berkshire Canal. This canal opened in 1810 and linked Abingdon via Wantage to the Kennet & Avon Canal, joining it at Semington in Wiltshire. It was always a rural canal although in its heyday it carried cheese from the Vale to London as well as coal from Somerset to Oxford. It was soon in competition with the railways and by the mid-nineteenth century had much reduced traffic, finally being closed in 1910.

Along the road on the left, notice the elm saplings growing from rootstock remaining after the death of the original trees from Dutch Elm disease. The saplings are too small to be attacked by the bark beetle which transmits the fungus causing the fatal disease. The elm leaves feel like coarse sandpaper and are food for a tiny burrowing mite which produces the numerous warts on the leaf surface.

In the woodland, follow the path straight ahead for 110 yards (100 m), then turn right at a junction of paths and continue to a stile at the edge of the wood.

The name of the woodland, Uffington Gorse, indicates that this area was once part of the common, and plants like gorse, bracken and rushes are remnants of its vegetation. Native trees – oak, cherry, rowan – have been planted by the Woodland Trust, a charity devoted to the management and protection of woodlands. The open nature of the area will gradually change as the planted trees and self-sown silver birch

Honeysuckle

Rosebay willow-herb

and willow mature. Many of the flowers present now will disappear unless glades and rides are created in the maturing wood. Insects associated with the plants provide food for birds, and small mammals can also find food and shelter often lacking in the fields. Sweet smelling honeysuckle trails over trees and shrubs, showing the reason for its old name of woodbine. Well-established honeysuckle is a food plant for the caterpillars of the White Admiral butterfly, uncommon now but which could be introduced into a protected woodland such as this. Rosebay willow-herb is easily recognized by its tall spikes of rosy-pink flowers in late July and August, followed by plumes of fluffy, white wind-blown seeds. It produces blue pollen which can be seen on bees visiting the flowers.

4 SU315900

Go over the stile at the woodland edge and turn right along the road. At the junction cross straight over and take the field path ahead.

The first section of the path follows the line of the parish boundary between Uffington and Baulking. The boundary hedge is much older than many others you will pass today and contains a mixture of tree and shrub species. Look out for field maple, elm, hawthorn, blackthorn or sloe, crab-apple and dogrose. The open ground at the base of the hedge allows goosegrass or cleavers to flourish. The seeds germinate in autumn and are frost resistant, so that the seedlings can grow quickly in spring. Tiny hooked hairs on the long shoots cling to other plants for support and the hard seeds are also covered with barbed hairs which cling to passing people and animals, so helping their dispersal. The bare ground in early summer warms quickly and butterflies such as small tortoiseshell and peacock may be seen basking in the sun.

After a quarter of a mile (0.5 km), the path crosses a straight drainage channel as it joins Stutfield Brook and then bears right across the field to the junction of the fence line and the band of trees.

93

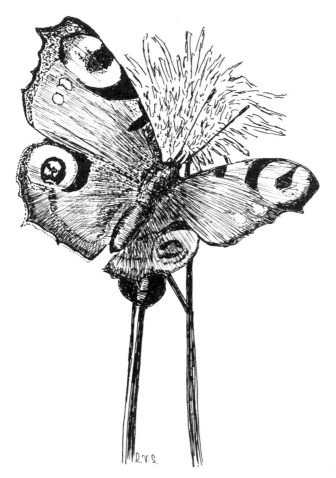

Peacock butterfly

When the path reaches Stutfield Brook see how the
vegetation changes with the damper conditions. Bur-
reed, great willow-herb and meadowsweet all like wet
ground, as do the Phragmites reeds along the stream.
Tansy with yellow button-like flowers can also be
found here. In the Middle Ages this plant was often
strewn on floors to keep flies and fleas away and now
it is found that the dried flowers contain a natural
insecticide related to pyrethrum. You may spot reed-
buntings here too; listen for their chattering song, quite
a contrast to the skylarks overhead. In these fields,

Tansey

notice the grey colour of the soil, especially when it has been freshly ploughed, characteristic of Gault Clay (see Introduction).

The line of trees and thick vegetation again marks the route of the Wiltshire & Berkshire Canal, which here is slightly more apparent. There used to be a swingbridge here but this has long since gone.

5   SU319891

Climb over the stile and continue straight on across the field to the road.

From the stile there is a wide view of the Downs and a glimpse of the White Horse. There is a marked contrast between the relatively damp agricultural fields and the dry chalky uplands. In the distant past parishes in this escarpment area evolved into long narrow shapes to take into their territory a mixture of land types so that the inhabitants had access to cultivatable land, water and dry grazing pasture. You may be able to pick out a pattern of terraces on the hillside ahead. These are called lynchets and are remnants of medieval cultivation, possibly formed during the twelfth or thirteenth centuries when the population was increasing and food production was under pressure. Lynchets are really extensions of the open fields onto steep ground, the terraces formed by plough action across the hillside. Further along this walk you will see remains of ridge-and-furrow cultivation which is the equivalent formation on level ground.

Turn left and walk to Fawler. Continue past Fawler Manor until you see a footpath signposted to the right, next to Fawler Cottage.

The wide roadside verges are attractive in summer with colourful flowers. Lady's bedstraw can be found with loose clusters of tiny yellow flowers. This plant is related to the cleavers seen earlier whose flowers are inconspicuous. Red clover and common vetch also grow here as well as goatsbeard. This plant has dandelion-type flowers which only open fully on sunny mornings, hence its other name of Jack-go-to-bed-at-noon. However, its seed-head is rather spectacular forming a large brown 'clock'.

Fawler is an old settlement with evidence of Roman occupation. Like Fawler in West Oxfordshire (see Book 1, *Evenlode and Wychwood*), the village gets its name from the Old English 'fagan flore' meaning mosaic pavement, obviously a relic from the days of the Romans. Like Uffington, Fawler also belonged to Abingdon Abbey. St James church was in existence early in the sixteenth century but after the dissolution of the monasteries by Henry VIII it fell into disuse and the site has now disappeared.

Sparrows are common around any domestic buildings; these opportunistic birds have done well out of their association with people. In summer, flocks of sparrows move into nearby hedgerows and fields to feed on cereals growing there, returning to gardens and farmyards after harvest. The male has a black bib under his chin, the size indicating how important he is within the local group. Dominant, high-ranking individuals have much larger bibs than the lesser males and their rank position determines access to food, water and nest sites.

6   SU320881

Take the path to the right beside Fawler Cottage, through a gate into a field. Head slightly to the left to a foot-bridge and small gate. Through this, head slightly right to a stile in a straggly hedge. Over the stile, go straight on, following a grassy track to a stile beside a gate. In the next field, bear left along the hedgeline to another gate and foot-bridge, then follow the path straight ahead over an arable field. At the end of this field is another bridge and stile. Once over this the main walk continues straight on.

If you want a short cut, turn right and follow the footpath back to Uffington, turning right at the road.

In some of the fields along this part of the walk, notice the mixture of grasses and flowering plants compared to some of the improved planted grassland seen earlier which are used for grazing and silage rather than hay. Red clover, buttercups and trefoils all add to the variety which animals prefer in hay, therefore their presence is beneficial.

Hedges and trees provide welcome shade for animals, especially for sheep with heavy fleeces in early summer, as well as shelter from wind and rain. Bare patches alongside show how frequently they are used by animals for these purposes.

Some fields show large ridges and furrows which are more noticeable when the grass is short or there is a scattering of snow. After heavy rain, the furrows are noticeably wetter than the ridges. These ridges are the result of medieval ploughing which gradually heaped up the soil to help drainage. Crops were grown on the ridges, groups of which formed the strips held by different villagers.

As you walk through cereal or rape fields, look at the 'weeds' growing there and notice that they are different in the two types of crops. Cereals are grasses so the weed-killer is chosen to destroy non-grass weeds; in rape fields the opposite occurs, and a selection of flowering plants like poppies, wild pansy and scarlet pimpernel may be seen. Another name for pimpernel is poor-man's weather glass since the flowers are open only in warm sunshine and close in damp or cool weather.

7 SU304881

When the path reaches the road, turn right for a few steps then take the path to the left over a stile. Continue across two fields, over a double stile. Then, close to a large oak tree, look out for a stile in the hedge on the right. Cross this and then carry on as before but now with the hedge on the left-hand side.

The bramble or blackberry bushes in the hedge are a good source of sustenance for many animals. Apart from the berries eaten by birds, small mammals and some insects, as well as man, the pinkish flowers in midsummer attract many butterflies including the striking red admiral with distinctive red and white markings on the dark wings. The leaves are food for the caterpillars of several moth species.

If you look up to the left here you will get a good view of the White Horse. This ancient symbol is cut through the turf into the natural chalk underneath and is thought to date from the late Iron Age, probably the late first century BC. Weathering and erosion has occurred over the centuries so the present shape may be different to that of the original horse. Every few years the horse was scoured when the outline was re-cut and generally tidied. This used to be the duty of the villages lying at the foot of the escarpment from Ashbury to Sparsholt in the Hundred of Hildeslow and gradually developed into a big public event with fairs, racing and cheese-rolling. A famous description was written by Thomas Hughes, author of *Tom Brown's Schooldays*, in 1857 when the event was revived. Now the White Horse is a scheduled ancient monument under the guardianship of English Heritage and is owned and managed by the National Trust. Visitors are asked to keep off the Horse to reduce erosion.

The path crosses the hedge beside a large oak tree which may have been used in the past as a marker for the parish boundary between Uffington and Woolstone, which crosses the path at this point, continuing up the escarpment towards the White Horse. Large trees were often mentioned in deeds or charters when boundaries were described.

8   SU295879

When the path reaches the road, turn left into Woolstone. Walk past cottages and houses, then at a junction close to the White Horse pub turn right and follow the road past more cottages to a sharp right-hand bend and out of the village.

The White Horse, Woolstone

As you walk, look at some of the plants along the walls and in the gardens. Aspen trees can be seen as you enter the village. The leaves have long stems which cause them to flutter in the slightest wind. This may be a device to discourage insect predators as they find it difficult to keep a foothold. Buddleia seedlings can be found in the stone walls. This decorative plant was introduced from China at the end of the nineteenth century and is well known as the 'butterfly bush' because of its attractiveness to these and other insects. Seedlings seem to thrive in dry stony places like walls and building sites where the high calcium content may be favourable to them. In rich garden soil, seedlings grow very slowly, often being eaten by slugs or swamped by other plants. In late spring you may notice a strong smell of garlic; look for a patch of white flowered ramsons under the trees on the right just past the stream.

The name of Woolstone comes from 'Walfric's tun',

a Saxon settlement, but with the White Horse so close there was obviously human habitation in the area much earlier. A Roman villa was discovered to the west in 1844 but there are no visible remains. In the Domesday Book, Woolstone was recorded as being held by the Bishop of Winchester to provide supplies for the monks. The church was built in 1195 but the windows are modern as the old ones were blown out by a Second World War bomb. Like Uffington, most of the old houses are built of chalk ashlar, but one building is markedly different. This is a red-brick tower, just uphill almost opposite the pub. It was built as a folly but was never completed – look for the date and initials in the brick-work.

If, when you reach the right-hand bend in the road, you continue for a short distance straight on along a path, over the hedge on the left you will see a very bumpy field full of nettles. These bumps are all that remains of house platforms, dating from the Middle Ages, showing how Woolstone has shrunk over the centuries. Nettles often grow in places where there was human or animal habitation. These plants recycle nitrogen from waste matter in the soil and so act as a good indicator of past use.

9 SU292877

After the right bend, continue along the lane, Marsh Way, until you reach a pond on the left-hand side of the road.

Marsh Way has wide verges containing a variety of calcium-loving plants such as mauve field scabious, purple knapweed, yellow lady's bedstraw and many others. Dark meadow-brown butterflies feed among the flowers in summer but their caterpillars are grass feeders. The male butterflies are much darker than the females which tend to be light brown or orange. The hedges are covered with climbing plants in places. Poisonous woody nightshade or bitter-sweet has purple and yellow flowers, like those of tomato, and red berries in autumn. Greater bindweed grows rampantly over the hedge with large trumpet-shaped white flowers; its older names of hedge lily or old man's nightcap reflect the flower shape rather than the growth habit. The pond is fringed by iris and sedges as well as grasses which in time will cause the pond to dry up if not regularly cleared. It is a refuge for moorhen and sometimes ducks which feed on the damselflies and other insects living here. In summer you may see an occasional large hawker dragon-fly. This is usually a male holding the pond as its territory. It will chase away other males while waiting for a female to come along. They hunt as they fly and grab other insects by the legs, then perch on a tall look-out point as they eat their catch.

Take the path to the right opposite the pond and follow it through this field. Make for the stile and foot-bridge ahead in the hedge to your right. (This may be hidden in undergrowth.) Cross this into another field. Continue in the same direction as before, now with the hedge on your left. Cross the double stile in the field corner. Take care as there is a ditch between the stiles. Go round the bushes to the left and follow the treeline. Walk over a small bridge and take the path behind the cottage alongside a stream. You will emerge onto a road.

In the fields past the pond you can find several members of the pea family: bird's foot trefoil, yellow vetchling and pink-flowered common vetch. These have complicated flowers which need to be pollinated by bees which can push past the petals. Flies and other insects do not do this. These plants can use nitrogen from the air to help with their nutrition, hence they grow well in poor soils. Clover is another member of this family and is often used as a green manure, being ploughed directly into the ground where it adds extra fertility to the soil.

At the junction beside the cottage, look up into the overhanging horse chestnut tree where you will see a clump of mistletoe. This parasitic plant is more commonly found on apple or poplar trees. Male and female flowers are borne on different plants, the sticky white berries appearing on the female plant. The sticky seeds are dispersed by birds wiping their beaks on tree branches. In the past mistletoe was thought to have magical properties in warding off witchcraft, and the surviving custom of kissing under the mistletoe is a relic of this.

10 SU295886

At the road there is a footpath sign on your left; take the right-hand path, diagonally right over a field. Continue to the end of the field, go over a bridge, stile and metal gate on the right, then follow the path diagonally across the field to a white fence and stile. Over the stile, turn right along the road until you reach a junction. Here turn left to another junction where you take the right fork. Continue along this road back to your starting point in Uffington.

Close to the last junction, you will pass a tiny chalk building, now the home of the Tom Brown's Schooldays Museum. This is open from Easter to October at weekends and bank holidays from 2 to 5 p.m. and on weekdays by appointment (tel: Uffington 820675 or 820318).

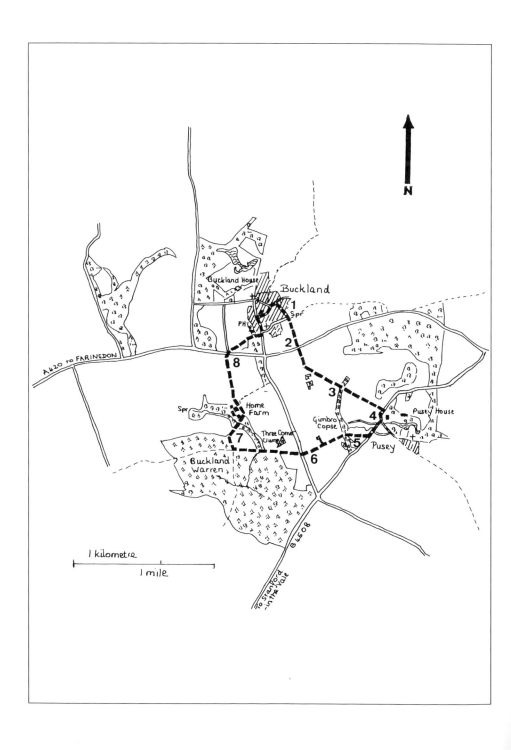

WALK 7
Buckland

3.5 miles   5.5 km

This is a level walk through a quiet landscape of fields and woods leading to Pusey, and returning to Buckland along easy tracks.

1 SU345980

Starting from the large car-park at Buckland Memorial Hall, turn right downhill to the stream and on to the end of the road.

Buckland gets its name from the Old English for 'an estate granted by royal charter', although when this happened is unknown. The major landowner by 1086 was the Bishop of Exeter. The Domesday Book records a dairy in his ownership which produced 10 weys of cheese, worth 32*s* 4*d* (£1.61), a wey being several hundredweight. Like many other villages in the area, part was owned by Abingdon Abbey, although Exeter's share was much greater.

Along the stone wall are numerous small cushions of moss, which are highly adapted to withstand low nutrient and moisture conditions. The long hairs give the plants their whitish colour and serve to retain moisture within the cushion. These mosses are home to a variety of microscopic worms, insects and other small animals, many of which have the ability to become inactive when very dry, returning to normal when wet.

Along the verge past the houses, the very large leaves belong to butterbur. The scientific name is derived from the Greek for hat, an apt description of the leaves which shade out any other plants beneath them. The pink clusters of flowers appear in spring before the leaves are developed. Most of the plants in this country produce male flowers, female plants only appearing in the north of England.

Where the road bends to the right, take the bridleway going straight ahead along the field edge.

Along the field path look out for pale yellow snails often with brown bands on them, as well as pink or dark brown forms. These are all the same species but the number of each colour varies in different places. In grassy areas, yellow-banded snails are very abundant, whereas in hedgerows and shady areas pink and brown are more common. This difference reflects how well they are camouflaged in different places and therefore how easily they are found by thrushes as food. The verge of the field contains many flowering plants, a contrast to the weed-free cereal crop. Yellow hedge mustard, white campion, pink mallow and cranes-bill are nectar sources for many insects which prey on cereal pests, thus the value in leaving these field verges unsprayed.

2   SU347975

When you reach the main road, cross with care to the gateway slightly to the right. Cross the stile and walk straight on along a slightly raised path following the hedge on your right. At the top of the field the path turns left in front of the farm buildings.

In the first field there are large clumps of thistles along the hedge bottom. Spear thistles have sharp spiny leaves, hence their name, whereas woolly thistle can be identified by the fine, white threads between the spines on the large flower-heads. Closer to the farm are two other thistles. One with small, pale mauve flowers often growing in clumps is creeping thistle, while the other has large, drooping flower-heads borne on stalks with small green 'wings'. There are two groups of thistles and these wings help identify the group to which the species belongs. Along the hedge you may see some large webs full of caterpillars. These are small ermine moth caterpillars which live in groups and spin the thick silk around themselves for protection. They will form the cocoon inside the silk when they are fully grown and ready to change into the small white moth.

The farm buildings are shielded by a line of limes with some horse-chestnuts at the far end. Horse-chestnut was introduced from Southern Europe, probably by the Romans. The newly opened flowers have a yellow spot in the centre, which soon changes to pink. This is a sign to insects that the flowers are ready for pollination. The limes attract insects by their

Mallow

strong smell and bees often get drunk on the rich nectar. Another plant which signals to insects is the pink-flowered mallow which grows near the next stile. The dark pink veins in the petals act as 'honey guides', directing visiting bees to the nectar at the base of the flower.

At the end of the trees where the farm vehicles churn up the ground you will find a selection of plants known as weeds of cultivation: docks, chickweed, fat-hen and mayweed. These plants grow quickly but need light open conditions for germination, hence they do not do well among other plants or grasses.

Continue to a stile, then bear diagonally to the right across the field, following the line of the overhead wires, to reach a stile at the far side of the field.

The path across the field follows the line of a well-marked route between Buckland and Pusey which is shown on maps made in the eighteenth and nineteenth centuries. Children from Pusey walked to school in Buckland at the end of the nineteenth century and early twentieth century and would have used this path every day. The land on which this field and farm now stand was described as common in 1761, the farm probably only being built after enclosure in 1803.

3   SU352971

At the edge of the field the path leads over a stile into a small copse.

The crumbling wall at the edge of Gimbro Copse marks the parish boundary between Buckland and Pusey. Just north of here its route zig-zags, as shown on a map made in 1761, indicating where the furlongs of the old open field ended.

Several of the trees in the copse are old and dying; notice how the top branches are leafless, producing the stag-headed appearance. Newly planted trees nearby will gradually enlarge the copse, enhancing its value for wildlife, particularly woodland and game birds. The new trees are all native species including oak, field maple, ash, cherry, hazel and rowan. When young they are protected by plastic Tully tubes which stop animals grazing on the young shoots as well as providing a mini-greenhouse to speed up growth.

Through the trees, continue along a track in the same direction as before to a stile onto the road.

Along the track, white campion and red field poppies grow in profusion. Both these plants spread their seeds in a similar way: the dry seed-case opens to allow the seeds to be shaken out by the wind like a pepper pot. Thistles and dandelions also rely on wind to disperse their seeds but these have parachutes of fine hairs which help them to float over a wider area away from the parent plant.

This large field was once the North Field of the Manor of Pusey. It was divided into furlongs which were then further subdivided into strips. Some of the furlong names can still be identified from old documents; this path passes between Picked Furlong, meaning a pointed piece of land, and Broadmoor Furlong, which lay next to Broadmoor in Buckland parish and was part of their common.

4   SU357968

At the road, first turn left for about 160 yards (150 m) to get a fine view of Pusey House, then retrace your steps and walk through Pusey village, following the road towards Gainfield. At the end of the houses and gardens look for a bridleway to the right.

Pusey is an ancient settlement. Its name means 'pea island', an indication of how wet this area was before modern drainage and water extraction. Tradition has it that the manor of Pusey was granted to William Pewse in 1015 by the Viking King Cnut on 'horn tenure' and an ancient horn was owned by the Pusey family for many centuries. The present house was built in 1750 for John Allen Pusey and was the birth place of Edward Bouverie Pusey, a leader of the nineteenth-century Oxford Movement which called for reform of the Church of England. Many of the cottages were built at the same time as the house, the old village and

Pusey House

some roads being remodelled to produce a more perfect setting.

In summer, look under the eaves of some of the houses for house-martins. They make their nests from wet mud which they collect at the edge of puddles, ponds or streams. Their nests are always placed high so that they can dive in and out of them. The small stream alongside the road used to be called Cress Ditch, inside the garden it has been dammed to form a lake.

5 SU355965

Take the bridlepath and follow this between a double fence and through a copse. Continue along a fieldpath to a road.

Out of the reach of grazing animals there is a fine display of flowering plants. Cowslips can be seen in spring; these plants suffered a considerable decline when fields were improved with artificial fertilizers as they cannot compete with fast-growing grasses and other plants. Now that fertilizer use is being reduced, cowslips are reappearing. Broad-leaved plantain grows in the centre of the path; its large, flat leaves all grow from the base of the stem, thus creating space for the plant and allowing it to tolerate trampling. Another plantain with narrow leaves is found in the taller vegetation at the side of the path. This is ribwort plantain, so named because of its prominent leaf veins. Look for bladder campion with more delicate white flowers than white campion and distinctive pale brown swellings at the base of each flower. Don't ignore the grasses; see how many different sorts grow here. They can easily be told apart when they are flowering.

Such a flowery path is a good home for grasshoppers and crickets. Early in summer the immature insects can be told from the adults by their lack of wings. Both types of insect belong to the order *Orthoptera*, which refers to the straight edges of the front wings. Grasshoppers use their strong legs to leap quite long distances but many crickets only crawl

Cricket (left), grasshopper (right)

through the vegetation. Grasshoppers have straight antennae but those of crickets curl back along the length of their body.

The path leads through Gimbro Copse again. Just to the south of here are some disused quarries which in the past would have supplied building stone for the village. The ground is moist under the trees and shrubs and this encourages plants like meadowsweet and hemp agrimony to flourish. Hawthorn, dogrose, elder and spindle make a dense undergrowth and all provide good food sources for insects, birds and mammals at different times of the year. Mice will even climb into rose, hawthorn and hazel bushes to eat the nuts and berries.

When you emerge from the copse, go quietly and you may see rabbits grazing in the fields. Look out too for long-eared and long-legged hares which are slightly larger than rabbits. Rather than running away, they will often crouch down to the ground, making them very hard to see.

There may be quite a variation in the crops you see along this walk. Until quite recently it was not feasible to grow maize successfully in this country as the summer season is too short. Plant breeders have developed new varieties, which can grow and reproduce faster so that they are now a useful crop, even though the difference in their growing season is only a few days.

Some interesting plants grow along the track here. Yellow flower-heads or umbels like those of cow-parsley, belong to wild parsnip, an ancestor of the cultivated vegetable. If you crush a leaf you will notice the sweetish parsnip smell, but be careful in handling it as some people react painfully to the chemicals on the leaves and stem, developing a severe rash. Another plant with a strong smell is mugwort. This large bushy plant has tiny flowers and soft, grey-green aromatic leaves, and in the past was used in bedding to discourage fleas. Orange-red soldier beetles can be found on many flower-heads, feeding on pollen and nectar. Their name comes from their colour which is like that of the old army uniforms.

6   SU348963

Cross the road and continue along the track alongside woodland until you reach a junction of tracks.

This track is a continuation of one seen in Walk 3 (Hatford), leading from Faringdon through Buckland Warren to Pusey and on to Charney Basset, hence its name Warren Road. Its route may have evolved over a long period as it follows slightly higher ground than that in the nearby Ock valley which, in the past, was quite marshy and difficult underfoot.

In 1761 all the land in this area was commonland but by 1820 many trees had been planted including the Three Corner Clump which you can still see on the right. Since then more trees have appeared, so that almost all the old commonland is now wooded. Ash grows first along the route, followed by a variety of conifers. Ash produces a lightweight wood, which is tough and elastic. It was used as handles for implements like brooms, pickaxes and oars which need wood with a certain amount of 'spring'. Three different conifers can be seen along the path. Austrian pine has dark-grey bark and is often planted as an ornamental tree as you will see later. Scots pine is a native tree and has orange bark towards the top of the trunk. It is a timber tree grown to provide telegraph poles, railway sleepers and building materials. The third conifer is Douglas Fir, named after David Douglas who introduced this species from Canada in

1827. The good quality timber is used in ship and house building, joinery and box making. Leaves or needles on fir trees grow singly on the branches whereas pine needles arise in clusters.

7 SU339964

At the junction of paths turn right, with woodland to the left and a field on the right. Keep right at the next intersection and walk through a small marshy copse, pass a stone dovecot on the right and farm buildings on the left. Continue along the track until you reach the road.

Viper's bugloss

Along this track, three members of the borage family can be found. Viper's bugloss has pink buds followed by bright blue flowers with long stamens protruding snake-like from the flower. Comfrey is a tall plant with white or mauve-pink flowers and hairy stems and leaves, like many members of this family. A now common relative, Russian comfrey was introduced into this country by Henry Doubleday at

Stone dovecot, Home Farm

Avenue of Austrian pines

the end of the nineteenth century, hoping to use its sticky sap for glue for postage stamps. This project foundered but it was discovered that the plant is a rich source of nitrogen and so its use as an organic garden fertilizer added to compost heaps or as a liquid extract has developed. Alkanet has very bright blue flowers, similar to forget-me-not which also belongs to this family. These latter two plants grow around the early nineteenth-century octagonal dovecot which was probably built at the same time as the woodland was planted. Past Home Farm, which pre-dates the dovecot, the track is lined with a fine avenue of Austrian pines, planted in threes at the same time as the other ornamental woodland passed earlier.

8 SU339974

At the main road, cross with care and take the path opposite through the stone gateposts. Go past the

Buckland House

lodge, then take a stile on the right. The path leads to the right across the field to another stile into woodland.

From this field, Buckland House can be seen. This mansion was built for Sir Robert Throckmorton in 1757, and substantially enlarged in about 1910. It replaced the older manor-house which was revamped into Gothick stables. The old deer park, which dated from at least the thirteenth century was redesigned by Lancelot 'Capability' Brown in 1760. A later member of the family, Sir John Throckmorton, became famous in 1811 for making a wager of 1,000 guineas that a coat could be made from wool sheared, spun, woven and dyed in a day. Two Southdown sheep were taken to Greenham Mill near Newbury at 5 a.m. one day and the coat was finished at 6.20 p.m. The dark blue Throckmorton coat used to be kept at the house but is now in the museum at Newbury.

This field has a park-like appearance with a scatter of old trees. Animals have grazed the lower branches making a browse line so that they look as if they have been carefully trimmed to give a flat base. Sheep and rabbits help to keep the turf in this field short and bouncy to walk on. Sheep, like other farm animals, have changed over the years reflecting changing needs of farmers and consumers. The Southdown sheep, used for the Throckmorton coat, was bred in the eighteenth century from sheep native to the Suffolk Downs and later became the basis of the Down breeds. Many of these are now rare, but the Suffolk breed, derived from Southdown, provide about half of all British rams, used mainly for cross-breeding. Over the years sheep have been bred to produce meat, milk and wool depending on market demands. Many ewes now frequently produce twins or triplets as a result of research breeding.

Follow the path through the woodland to the road and turn left. Walk until you see The Lamb public house set back on your left. Turn right opposite and follow the road back through the village to the starting point.

After you leave the woodland, notice the mixture of plants growing at the foot of many garden walls. Garden and wild flowers grow together, sometimes from the same botanical family. Wild blue meadow cranes-bill is common on many road verges in Oxfordshire while the purple-crimson bloody cranes-bill is native to the limestone dales in the north of England and here grows as a garden plant.

Meadow cranes-bill

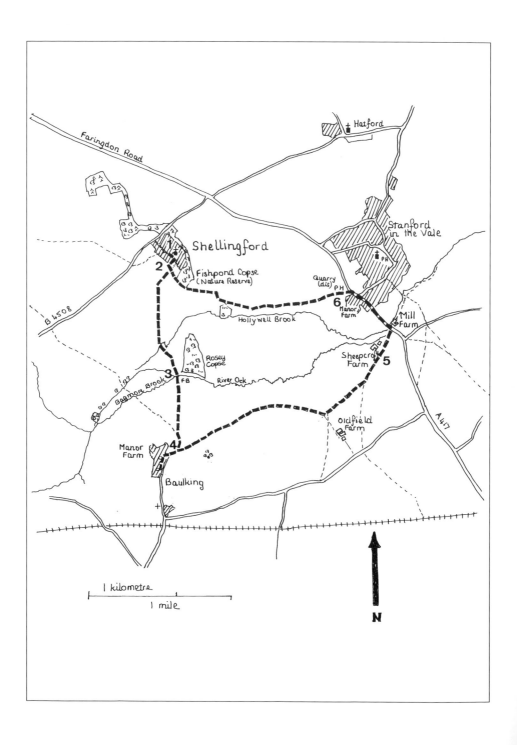

Faringdon Road

Shellingford

Fishpond Copse
(Nature Reserve)

Hatford

Stanford
in the Vale

PH

Quarry
(dis)
PH

B 4508

Hollywell Brook

Rosey
Copse

River Ock

Baggmor Brook

FB

Manor
Farm

6
Manor
Farm

Mill
Farm

Sheepcrot
Farm

5

Oldfield
Farm

A 417

Baulking

1 kilometre
1 mile

N

Shellingford

5.5 miles   9 km

This is a level walk from Shellingford through the Ock valley, skirting Baulking and Standford-in-the-Vale. There are wide views to the Berkshire Downs in the south and Faringdon Folly to the north-west. Some parts through ploughed fields will be strenuous in wet weather.

1   SU319935

Start from the village street in Shellingford close to the church and walk away from the main road (B4508). Just past the church take the path on the right, opposite the school, through a farmyard. Follow the arrows around the buildings to emerge onto a track.

The name of Shellingford reflects the once very wet nature of this landscape. There are many places with 'ford' in their names in this area – how many can you see on the map? The manor belonged to Abingdon Abbey before the Domesday Book was made in 1086. There was much meadow for haymaking and obviously dairy products were a large part of their economy with dues from cheese worth £4 16s 8d (£4.83). The church is worth a visit and has a good example of a Norman doorway with a typical dog-tooth pattern decorating its round arch. Just south of the church once stood Shellingford Castle, the site of the old manor-house, now just a farmyard and grass.

Shellingford church

The line of cottages next to the church were probably offices for the manor.

Old-fashioned single hollyhocks grow by the cottage walls. These large open flowers are great favourites with bees who get covered in the copious pollen. The horticultural practice of making many types of plant double flowered often reduces their value for insects as pollen and nectar supplies are drastically reduced. Notice how the leaf shape varies on different plants, some being large and broad while others have lobed leaves like stubby fingers. This difference is inherited and very easy to breed for.

Jackdaws fly around the church and farm buildings. They are smaller than rooks or crows and have distinctive grey heads. Large buildings in rural areas provide them with ideal nest sites. Another bird which is often associated with human habitation is the collared dove, a pretty soft-grey bird with a black band around its

Collared dove

neck. This species spread across Europe in the twentieth century and reached Britain only a few decades ago. Living close to people, they have successfully established themselves, like sparrows and jackdaws, finding good food supplies around habitations.

In the garden of the farm notice the staddle-stones in the garden. These were used in the past as supports for grain stores. The stones kept the store above wet ground and the overhanging mushroom tops prevented rodents from getting into the grain.

2 SU319934

Ignoring the first stile on the left, continue along the track for the length of a field until you pass a hedge. Here, turn left through a gate and follow the path diagonally right across the field to a gap in the trees.

Many of the hedges in this fieldscape are very gappy and neglected and do not provide an effective barrier for stock. In this state they are of no real benefit to wildlife either. Dogroses grow along the hedgeline; the flowers are good for insects in summer while the red autumn hips provide food for birds and mice. In most plants the male pollen and female egg each contribute half the genetic inheritance material, but in these plants the male pollen only contributes 20 per cent.

The thick band of trees provides plenty of shelter for cattle as well as wildlife. The large oak tree beside the stile has wide spreading branches, quite a different shape to a woodland oak which tends to have fewer side branches but a large crown at the top where the leaves have light. It is covered in ivy, the stems thick and old. There seems to be mixed opinion as to whether ivy damages trees; certainly it clings for support but does not take any nutrition from the tree, and is really only a problem on dying trees. The evergreen leaves provide winter shelter for owls, wrens and other birds while the black berries are winter food eaten by pigeons and blackbirds. The flowers, produced in late autumn, are a vital nectar source for many insects such as flies and wasps.

Go through a gate and follow the path in the same direction as before to a stile. This path may be mown through the crop. Over the stile, bear very slightly left to the stile ahead beside a willow tree. This stile is between two gates. Keeping the fenceline on the right, continue to another stile, then straight on to a stile and foot-bridge.

The wood across to the left, Rosey Copse, has been in existence for at least 250 years, although its shape has changed over time. Many of the trees in the copse have dead tops, the so-called stag-head effect. The reason for their dying off may be one or more of many. However, one reason is that ploughing may damage roots near the surface of the soil.

Pheasants shelter in the woods but can often be seen looking for food in the fields. Flocks of rooks are also common, feeding on insects in the grass.

Black and white friesian cattle may be grazing in the fields. Notice how the pattern of each coat is different. These patterns are just like human fingerprints in that they are completely individual, although those of close relatives tend to look similar. The cow-pats in these fields are a hive of activity. When very fresh, they are attractive to yellow dung flies. The male arrives first and takes up position on the pat, ready to lay claim to a female. The males fight for possession of a female and the winner sits on her back as she lays her eggs ensuring that no other male can mate with her. As the pat dries, a hard crust forms on it and small dung-beetles have to dig their way in – you can see the holes they make. All these insects serve the very useful function of breaking up the rich dung-pat so that its nutrients can be released back into the soil.

Other fields may be sown with silage grass which will be cut several times over the summer season. The cut grass is fermented in clamps or polythene-covered bales to make a nutritious winter food for cattle. The grass is thick and lush and quite difficult to walk through. Sometimes, depending on the season, a hay crop may be taken from the same fields. In this country today, much hay is made from specially sown grass with few flowers, but in the Alps and other places in Europe, hay is still made using a mixture of grasses and plants which add to its palatability and quality.

3   SU319922

Cross the stile and foot-bridge over the River Ock. Head across the field to the line of trees and a track.

Here the river is still no more than a stream but its flowing water provides a different habitat to the still water in ditches. Look out for metallic blue damselflies with a large black spot on the wings and also for metallic green damselflies with brown wings. These species are only found near running water while other species are not so choosy. Damselflies are more delicate and smaller than dragon-flies and fold their wings over their backs whereas dragon-flies hold them horizontally when at rest.

Continue on the footpath through the next field and through a gap in the hedge, keeping the farm buildings to the right. Continue straight on through a green gate onto Baulking green.

Look back across the fields and you will be able to see Faringdon Folly on the hilltop about 3 miles (5 km) away as the crow flies (see Walk 3).

Along this path, the hedge and verge on the left are rich in species which in turn encourage a rich insect life. In summer look for marbled-white, hedge-brown and meadow-brown butterflies feeding on the bramble flowers, thistles and knapweed. All these butterflies are related and have caterpillars which feed on grasses. Marbled-whites and meadow-browns like open grassland but hedge-browns prefer field edges and hedgerows. Bees also like these flowers and the bumble-bees can be identified by their red-tailed, white-tailed or buff-tailed coloration. Their thick hairy coats allow them to be active earlier in the year than other bees. The very large queens coming out of hibernation have to start a new colony; they build their nest and collect food on their own until the first workers are raised which then take over these tasks. Their nests are much smaller than those of honey bees with many fewer individuals.

4   SU319912

At the end of the line of willows look for a bridleway sign to the left and follow the arrows over the fields.

Diversion to Baulking

Follow the track as it bears to the right across the open grassland to the road which leads through the village. Retrace your steps to rejoin the walk at the start of the bridleway signs.

Baulking is an ancient settlement. The earliest documentary mention of the village was in a charter of AD 948, in which King Eadred granted five hides of land to his servant Cuthred. It is now a very small settlement but in the past it seems to have been a thriving community with a market which took place on Thursdays until 1219 and Tuesdays thereafter, although it had died out by the eighteenth century. Baulking is recognized by historians as a fine example of an open-sided green village, one of the best in the country. The village now occupies only the west side of the green, with several buildings having disappeared since the Tithe map was made in 1840. There are signs that there were once houses on the east side as well, with many earthworks in the grass there. The green was used as a stinted common which means that only a specified number of animals were allowed to graze there. The rights were probably originally linked to occupation of a particular dwelling but in recent years it seems that they can be sold separately. Manor Farm had grazing rights for thirty-four sheep; rights for eight sheep were equivalent to that for one cow. Another use of the common was for digging clay, a pit being situated close to Hyde Farm.

Follow the bridleway across the field to a foot-bridge over a stream.

The hillock to your right is part of the spoil-heap from a quarry which produces fuller's earth. This very fine clay probably originated from water-borne sediments of volcanic material eroded from older land masses. Fuller's earth has been used for centuries as a

Baulking village scene

cleanser and whitener for wool, stripping away the natural grease, a process known as fulling. Today it is often processed to change its chemical composition, so making bentonite. This bentonite clay is found naturally in the USA and its ability to swell when mixed with water makes it useful in industry. It is used in the oil and construction industries as a drilling fluid, for sealing reservoirs and in the foundry industry in sand moulds. Extraction started here in 1980 by excavation to expose the fuller's earth, so forming the hillock. As the clay is removed so the trench is refilled and reseeded to return the land to agriculture. When all the fuller's earth has been taken, the earth forming the hillock will be placed in the final excavation but will not fill it due to the quantity of clay removed. A lake will form in the depression, which will be landscaped and planted with trees around its margin to form an attractive feature for the future.

Continue in the same direction over the brow of the hill and to a small gate in the hedge ahead.

This hill may be the site of the earliest settlement in Baulking as Iron Age and Romano-British evidence has been found here. Some of the hedges in this part of the walk have been grubbed out to enlarge the fields for greater efficiency in the use of large farm machinery. Other fields in the vicinity may now be in the set-aside scheme which has come about as a result of this efficiency in crop production.

Continue to a bridge and follow the arrow diagonally right across the next field to a gap in the hedge. Through the hedge, turn left and follow the hedge on your left-hand side, going from stile to stile.

Parallel to this path beyond the road runs the railway line. This was the Great Western main line built in 1840 from London to Bristol, the route chosen by its engineer, Isambard Kingdom Brunel.

Opposite Oldfield Farm the hedge-bank contains a succession of members of the carrot family or umbellifers, named for the umbrella shape of the flower-heads. Cow-parsley, with finely divided leaves, flowers first in April, followed in June and July by hogweed which is a coarser plant with lobed leaves. The delicate pinkish-white flowers of upright hedge-parsley do not appear until July. Two other members of the carrot family which both flower in late summer are often confused. Wild angelica has purplish stems and oval serrated-edged leaflets while the poisonous hemlock has purple spotted stems and finely divided fern-like leaflets.

5   SU342923

The path skirts to the right of Sheepcroft Farm. Continue diagonally left towards the corner of the field to a stile beside a small group of trees close to a cottage. The path leads to the road over another stile. At the road turn left towards Stanford-in-the-Vale. (If you wish to visit the village, take the next turning to the right. Retrace your steps later to return to the trail.)

At the Horse and Jockey pub take the footpath to the left, following the sign.

Stanford is another village with a 'ford' name, this time a stone ford. Here the River Ock is large enough to power water-mills and one of two recorded in the Domesday Book still exists at Mill Farm. Like Baulking, there used to be a market here in the thirteenth century. Later Stanford was famed for its speciality sage-flavoured cheese which was moulded into the shape of a hare. The road itself was made into a turnpike between Wallingford and Faringdon in 1752 during the reign of George II.

6 SU338931

Past the Horse and Jockey, follow the path over the stile at the end of the field, straight on to a foot-bridge and stone stile in the hedge.

Not far from the pub, notice how a most useful wildlife refuge has been created, with a pond, an area of rough meadow and a flower-rich strip of grassland bordering a recreation field. In midsummer, field scabious, ox-eye daisy, bird's foot trefoil and sainfoin with spikes of pink flowers attract a variety of butterflies including skippers. These differ from the usual butterfly shape in having triangular wings. You may also see the occasional painted lady, a migrant which comes to England from North Africa each year.

Continue straight on to another stile and bridge. Cross this field to a bridge and stile at the far right corner, crossing into the next field. Head for the stile in the centre of the far fence. Cross the track and the next stile. Continuing in the same direction, head for the left corner of the copse which you can see ahead. The path crosses a wide foot-bridge over a stream and leads into the edge of the wood – Fishpond Copse.

When you cross the foot-bridge at Fishpond Copse, look down at the waterside plants. You will see two which have very similar leaves. Watercress has four-petalled white flowers and long seed-pods, typical of a member of the cabbage family. This plant, rich in calcium and vitamins, is still grown commercially in the pure water of Letcombe Brook not far away near Wantage. Fool's watercress, which has an unpleasant bitter taste, has clusters of tiny white flowers and is another member of the carrot family like those you saw earlier.

Fishpond Copse, now a village nature reserve, is so named because it originated as a series of artificial fish-ponds taken off Holywell Brook which runs through Shellingford to join the Ock near Mill Farm.

Painted lady

The ponds may be medieval and were shown on an estate map made in 1778 and on the 1840 Tithe map.

After about 11 yards (10 m) the path bears left through a field-gate where it leads to a gateway, then right towards a farm. The trail goes left over the fence, then right at the stile onto the track where the walk started. Follow the arrows round the farmyard and return to the start.

Acknowledgements

This book was written and researched by Mary Webb, Alan Spicer and Allister Smith, all of Oxford Brookes University, and was illustrated by Louise Spicer.

The authors are grateful for help and support from the Centre for Oxfordshire Studies, Berkshire, Buckinghamshire and Oxfordshire Naturalists' Trust (BBONT), Oxford Fieldpaths Society, Alan Childs for advice on geology, and Barbara Southall for photographic assistance.

The project was sponsored by Oxfordshire County Council, Vale of White Horse District Council and Oxford Brookes University.

Vale *of White Horse*